"*Tested in Every Way* brings together a veritable cornucopia of voices, rich in intelligence and experience, about the Roman Catholic priesthood. Christopher Ruddy has done us all a service in fashioning these voices into a book which is lively and interesting."

— *Howard P. Bleichner, S.S.,*
author of View from the Altar

"Christopher Ruddy's *Tested in Every Way* embodies the true spirit of the Catholic Common Ground Initiative. With keen insight and great generosity, Ruddy reports on the 2003 Common Ground conference on 'The Priest in the Church' and gently draws the reader into a candid conversation about the state of the ordained priesthood today. Ruddy's own conclusions push past old debates toward a profoundly relational and Christ-centered vision. The book is a welcome call for the 'fresh eyes and changed hearts' needed to overcome present divisions and imagine future renewal in the ministerial life of the church."

— *Edward P. Hahnenberg, author of*
Ministries: A Relational Approach

"The need for competent and committed Catholic clergy is forcefully brought to light by Christopher Ruddy's book. Even in the age of the laity, there is no substitute for the spiritual leadership of priests and bishops."

—*Msgr. Charles Murphy, author of*
Belonging to God

"Chronicling a major conference of highly qualified speakers, Christopher Ruddy gives a lucid
account of the challenges that Catholic priests
face in our day. Bringing many different voices
into a constructive conversation, the book significantly enriches the body of Catholic literature on
priestly ministry."

— *Avery Cardinal Dulles, S.J.*

"*Tested in Every Way* justifies—in every way—the
late Cardinal Joseph Bernardin's conviction that
Catholics can find firm and common ground if
only they will listen to each other. Christopher
Ruddy's harmonizing of a wide range of voices,
themes, and concerns about the Catholic priesthood is exemplary in its depth and bracing in its
clarity. Anyone who fears for the future of the
church and its priests will find in these pages
much to think about, much to celebrate—and
much to do."

— *Kenneth L. Woodward,*
Contributing Editor, Newsweek

"This book gives us the pleasure and privilege of
listening into the conversation of the participants
of the conference, 'The Priest in the Church.' One
is caught up into a dialogue that is realistic, truth-
ful, and loving and in which people are unafraid
to face all the tough questions around the future
of the priesthood. It is a hopeful book which carries one beyond the usual polarities of 'left' and
'right' towards a vision of the Church and priesthood in which we may all be at home. Christopher Ruddy manages both to let a whole variety of

voices speak, and also offer a highly intelligent analysis and commentary that helps us both to see the challenges and also glimpse a way forward. We finish with a vision of the priesthood, focused on the Eucharist, that respects both the uniqueness of this vocation and its deep rootedness in the community of the people of God."

—*Timothy Radcliffe, O.P., former master general of the Dominican Order and author of* What Is the Point of Being a Christian?

"This is an invaluable book for those uneasy regarding the state of clergy–laity relationships in the Catholic Church. Christopher Ruddy expertly distills the wisdom of scholars and the real-life experiences of pastoral workers, as well as church documents and scripture, so that priests and lay people can better understand one another. Ruddy is uncanny in identifying the contours of the priesthood's current crisis. If his recommendations for an authentic priestly renewal are not heeded, it will be a serious tragedy and missed opportunity for grace."

— *Paul Stanosz, author of* The Struggle for Celibacy

TESTED
in
EVERY WAY

TESTED
in
EVERY WAY

Christopher Ruddy

A Herder & Herder Book
The Crossroad Publishing Company
New York

The Crossroad Publishing Company
481 Eighth Avenue, New York, NY 10001

This book emerged from a conference sponsored by the Catholic Common Ground Initiative. Catholic Common Ground is a division of the National Pastoral Life Center.

This book is set in 12/15 Garamond Premier Pro.
The display type is Brioso Pro Light.

Printed in the United States of America

Library of Congress Cataloging-in-Publication

Ruddy, Christopher, 1970-
    Tested in every way / by Christopher Ruddy.
        p. cm.
    Includes bibliographical references.
    ISBN-13: 978-0-8245-2427-2 (alk. paper)
    ISBN-10: 0-8245-2427-6 (alk. paper)
    1. Priesthood. 2. Priests. 3. Catholic Church—Clergy. 4. Pastoral theology—Catholic Church. I. Catholic Common Ground Initiative. II. Cardinal Bernardin Conference (7th : 2003 : San Antonio, Tex.) III. Title.

    BX1913.R83 2006
    262'.142—dc22

                                        2006024396

        1 2 3 4 5 6 7 8 9 10   12 11 10 09 08 07 06

In Memory of

Cardinal Joseph Bernardin
April 2, 1928 – November 14, 1996

Reverend Monsignor Philip Murnion
March 1, 1938 – August 19, 2003

"For we do not have a high priest
who is unable to sympathize with our weaknesses,
but we have one who in every respect has been tested
as we are, yet without sin."
Hebrews 4:15

Contents

The Priest: One "Set Apart" and "Like Us"

"**A**re you God?" When the priest told of being asked this question by a small child in his parish, many of the lay people present laughed. Most of the priests, though, nodded knowingly, some even wearily. The priest who told this story went on to say that victims of clerical sexual abuse will sometimes cry out, "God did this to me." Such anger and hurt arise because there is a sense—owing, among other things, to his attire, his ministry, his celibacy—that the Catholic priest is distinctively related to God. He is, to use a celebrated and contentious phrase, an icon of Christ. Although not intrinsically any holier or better than his fellow believers, he does capture the imagination in an unparalleled manner. If many people still have romantic or unrealistic conceptions of the Catholic priest (of which a reading of J. F. Powers's novels and short stories would disabuse them), it is clearer than ever that the priest is also deeply human, capable of great good and evil. This yoking of grandeur and misery should come as no surprise to the reader of scripture or church history—or, for that matter, to the congregation at any Mass.

Yet it seems that the church still struggles to come to terms with the vision of the priesthood as set forth in the Letter to the Hebrews—that lengthy, dense, and allusive work still sometimes mistakenly attributed to Paul. Timothy Radcliffe, the former head of the Dominican order, has written that Hebrews reveals a fuller vision of priesthood and of holiness: separation gives way to identification. Where older understandings of holiness stressed ritual purity and distance from the profane, Hebrews reveals Christ as the high priest and mediator who is holy precisely in embracing the brokenness and sinfulness of humanity. The letter, of course, offers a classically "high" vision of the holiness of Christ the high priest: he is "holy, blameless, undefiled, separated from sinners, and exalted above the heavens" (Hebrews 7:26). But, to a degree unequalled in the New Testament, it also emphasizes his radical humanity: "Since, therefore, the children share flesh and blood, he himself likewise shared the same things. . . . For it is clear that he did not come to help angels, but the descendants of Abraham. Therefore he had to become like his brothers and sisters in every respect" (2:14, 16–17).

This great high priest's holiness consists in embracing those marginalized, dispirited, tempted, stigmatized. He dies outside the city walls of Jerusalem, disgraced and outcast. He reconciles not with animal offerings but with his own blood on the cross and in the Eucharist. "Because he himself was tested by what he suffered, he is able to help those who are being tested" (2:18). His weakness reveals his strength, and his humanity is perfected in suffering.

This is the paradox of the priest as well: he is both "set apart" and "like us." He is able to heal his people because he represents Christ who is "the reflection of God's glory and the exact imprint of God's very being, and he sustains all things by his powerful word" (1:3), and yet he is "able to deal gently with the ignorant and wayward, since he himself is subject to weakness" (5:2). The tension between these two poles gives life to the priesthood but intensifies its trials. The clerical sexual-abuse scandals of recent years are only the most visible of these trials. It is no exaggeration to state, following Hebrews, that priests have been "tested in every way" (4:15) by what they have suffered. It may also be no exaggeration to state that such suffering might transform priests, leading them closer to Christ and his body. But it will do so only if priests and the whole church realize the gravity of their predicament.

The Conference

It was to address such a predicament that the Catholic Common Ground Initiative convened their Seventh Annual Cardinal Bernardin Conference, "The Priest in the Church," which brought together nearly fifty participants at the Oblate School of Theology in San Antonio from February 28 to March 2, 2003. They were bishops, priests, deacons, religious, and laity; white, black, Latino/a, and Asian; pastoral ministers, theologians, historians, community organizers, and spouses; ranging in age from thirty-two to beyond the biblical "three score and ten."

They gathered at a difficult time for the Catholic Church and its priests. It was barely a year beyond the symbolic beginning of the clerical sexual-abuse crisis on January 6, 2002—the day that the *Boston Globe* ran its first article on decades of priestly sexual abuse and episcopal dereliction in the Boston archdiocese. It was only a few months after the resignations of Cardinal Bernard Law of Boston and Archbishop Rembert

Weakland of Milwaukee—a charter member of the Initiative's advisory committee. And many priests felt mistrustful of, and betrayed by, their bishops at the United States Conference of Catholic Bishops' (USCCB) annual meeting in Dallas in June 2002, where they considered their rights to due process and a good reputation to have been jettisoned by bishops seeking to appease the court of public opinion through the adoption of a "zero tolerance" policy toward sexual abuse. Other priests, while often receiving the support and affection of their parishioners, nonetheless deemed that their collective integrity and dignity had been swept away by the crimes of a small minority of fellow priests.

This dark atmosphere hung over the conference and shaped its conversations, even when unmentioned. Over three days the conference participants explored the Catholic priesthood from a variety of perspectives: the contemporary ecclesial and cultural contexts for the priesthood; the concrete experience of priests today; the priest's relationships to God, his bishop or superior, his brother priests, the laity, his own self; and the initial and continuing formation of priests. Throughout, the conference took as its guiding question: "As the church moves forward, what does a good priest look like?"

The conference took up each of these perspectives in eight, roughly ninety-minute sessions (and in informal conversations at meals, breaks, and social gatherings). The participants had been sent seven papers as preparatory reading:

Scott Appleby, "Defending 'Truth,' Negotiating Pluralism, Evoking Hope: Once and Future Challenges to the Priesthood."

Cyprian Davis, O.S.B., "Development of the Theology of

Chastity and Priesthood: Mandatory Celibacy for Priests in the Early Church and at the Beginning of the Middle Ages."

Gerald Fogarty, S.J., "Priests and Their Bishops and People in the American Church."

Enda McDonagh, "The Risk of Priesthood."

Katarina Schuth, O.S.F., "Vocations, Seminarians, Initial Formation, and Continuing Education/Ongoing Formation for Priests: Some Information and Questions."

Susan Wood, S.C.L., "The New Intra-ecclesial Context for an Understanding of Priesthood Today."

Dean Hoge prepared a paper on "Characteristics of Priests in 2001," but did not attend the conference.

Each of the sessions began with some remarks on a designated topic by a previously chosen speaker or speakers, followed by a brief response where necessary from the paper's author. The floor was then opened up for comments, and each segment concluded with a brief summary by an assigned participant. Faithful to the Initiative's founding vision that the "fresh eyes and changed hearts" needed for renewed Catholic common ground could emerge only "in the space created by praise and worship," the conference was rooted in prayer, which included morning and evening prayer, as well as Mass.

The conversation that emerged from the conference focused more on priestly identity and relationships than on ministry and structures; who the priest *is* took precedence over what he *does*. While there clearly can be no separation of priestly identity and ministry, as the priest's ministry shapes his personal identity, nonetheless the participants mainly shared the conviction that the key issues facing priests today are relational ones: the priest *is* his relationships. In this regard, perhaps the most impassioned conversation arose over the priest's relationship to Christ and to his parishioners: How do the priest and his people form each other? How helpful is it to describe the priest as an icon of Christ? How does the priest's ongoing struggle as a disciple shape his ministry? Another set of relational issues centered on priests' relationships with one another: How do they deal with ambition and envy in the presbyterate? How do they negotiate their relationship with their bishop, who, as Vatican II emphasized, is both their father and their brother?

Accordingly, this relational emphasis meant that such contentious issues as the ordination of married men or of women were barely raised. I would add that this orientation was a fruitful one, as it allowed the participants to get at the heart of the Catholic priest and priesthood. While, as with any conference, there were repetitions and tangents and even the occasional posturing, a solid core of insight into the priesthood emerged from the discussions, and it is that core that this book will explore in the hope of fostering common ground in the church.

The Catholic Common Ground Initiative: Past, Present, and Future

The Catholic Common Ground Initiative was launched by the late Cardinal Joseph Bernardin of Chicago on August 12, 1996. It grew out of a several-years-long series of informal conversations among Catholic leaders and thinkers on contemporary pastoral priorities that were organized by the cardinal and the late Monsignor Philip Murnion, founder and director of the National Pastoral Life Center (NPLC) in New York City.

That day, the Initiative issued a statement, *Called to Be Catholic: Church in a Time of Peril*, which identified:

(1) key challenges facing American Catholicism, such as the increasing polarization among leaders in the church, both clerical and lay; the growing alienation and inadequate formation of many believers, especially among the young; the identity and future of Catholic institutions in such areas as education, health care, and social services;

(2) neuralgic issues that the church finds difficult to address openly and honestly, such as the changing roles of women, and the quality and effectiveness of religious education and of liturgy;

(3) the urgent need for dialogue in the church on said issues, and for such dialogue to be accountable to Christ and his church; particularly noteworthy is the statement's declaration that "Jesus Christ, present in Scripture and sacrament, is central to all that we do; he must always be the measure and not what is measured"; and

(4) working principles of an ecclesial dialogue that seeks to engage disagreement constructively and faithfully, so as to overcome polarization and renew the church's members and mission.

The Initiative and *Called to Be Catholic* attracted immediate attention, most of it supportive, even effusive. Neither has been without critics, though, both friendly and unfriendly.

Theologians such as then-Father Avery Dulles and David Schindler raised early questions about whether the Initiative's understanding of dialogue was too beholden to largely procedural models that implicitly bracketed the church's binding truth claims and its teaching authority; Schindler, in particular, wished that the statement had proposed a deeper, more explicitly christological and ecclesial conception of dialogue. (Significantly, both Dulles and Schindler have since participated in the Initiative's activities, the former as the 2001 annual lecturer and the latter as a participant in the Cardinal Bernardin Conferences.) Others thought that the perennial need for church renewal to be grounded in the call to holiness and conversion in Christ was obscured. Still others, admittedly a minority, thought that the Initiative was insufficiently inclusive of diverse viewpoints, particularly in regard to the priestly ordination of women.

Most strikingly, four of Cardinal Bernardin's fellow American cardinals—Anthony Bevilacqua of Philadelphia (now retired); James Hickey of Washington, D.C. (now deceased); Bernard Law of Boston (now resigned); and Adam Maida of Detroit—publicly criticized the Initiative within days and even hours of its announcement. Their criticisms matched those of other commentators—*Called to Be Catholic* played down the church's common ground in scripture and tradition, some claimed, or lacked emphasis on Christ as the key to ecclesial renewal—but their swift, public rebuke of a fellow cardinal was unprecedented and unmistakable. It bore, as Peter Steinfels notes in *A People Adrift*, the marks of a concerted effort to stop the Initiative.

Cardinal Bernardin patiently and clearly responded to these concerns in both a press statement and a public lecture.

Called to Be Catholic, he held, clearly upheld the primacy of scripture and tradition in any effort to foster common ground. He likewise denied that the statement placed church teaching and dissent on equal footing. In fact, it clearly stated the accountability of dialogue to the "living magisterium of the church exercised by the bishops and the chair of Peter." Finally, the statement's very first paragraph affirmed that "common ground [must be] centered on faith in Jesus," and, at the beginning of its section proposing a solution to polarization, it professed the centrality of Jesus to every effort of the Initiative: "He must always be the measure and not what is measured."

Thus, despite criticism and, more significantly, Cardinal Bernardin's death from pancreatic cancer in November 1996, the Initiative went forward and held its inaugural conference in March 1997. In the decade since its founding, the Initiative has been guided by an episcopal chair—Archbishop Oscar Lipscomb of Mobile assumed leadership during Cardinal Bernardin's final illness and was succeeded in 2003 by Archbishop Daniel Pilarczyk of Cincinnati—and a coordinator, Catherine Patten, R.S.H.M., of the NPLC. The chair and coordinator work with an advisory committee of over thirty Catholic leaders drawn from academia, business, law, and the church. Some of its more prominent members include Mary Ann Glendon of Harvard Law School and the Vatican's Academy of Social Sciences, Cardinal Roger Mahony of Los Angeles, and Judge John Noonan of the United States Court of Appeals, Ninth Circuit.

The Initiative presently conducts several programs. Its first major project is its annual Cardinal Bernardin Conference; past themes have ranged from church authority to young adult Catholics to the ongoing wisdom of Catholic sexual teaching. Its second effort is its annual lecture (named, since 2005, "The Philip J. Murnion Lecture"), delivered in Washington, D.C. Past speakers, along with Cardinal Dulles, have included Cardinal Walter Kasper of the Pontifical Council for Promoting Christian Unity and the late Cardinal Basil Hume of Westminster (London). Less formally, the Initiative also sponsors conferences and programs at various institutions. One notable result is the book *The Church Women Want* (Herder & Herder), edited by Elizabeth Johnson, C.S.J., and including contributions by Mary Ann Glendon and the theologian Diana Hayes of Georgetown University (all members of the Initiative's advisory committee). Most broadly, the Initiative seeks to provide guidance and support for efforts at all levels to promote reconciliation and unity in the church.

In its decade of existence, the Initiative has had mixed results. Its successes are notable. At the most basic level, it has surmounted denial and wishful thinking to draw attention to the existence and the corrosive effects of ecclesial polarization; naming a problem is often the first step in overcoming it. More deeply, it has fostered a high level of theological, spiritual, and pastoral conversation. To be blunt, it has kept faithful, respectful, intelligent, and candid conversation alive in times when such conversation has been in short supply in the church. As a participant in several of the annual conferences, I can attest to the difficulty and the fruitfulness of the faithful dialogue practiced there. It can be hard to trust those with whom one disagrees (or, even, considers profoundly wrong), to engage those of differing views not with wariness or suspicion, but with the friendship due to brothers and sisters in Christ. For all of one's noble words and hopes, old habits die hard. But, through the power of divine grace and human response, such habits can begin to dissolve. Only the passage of time will reveal the fruits of such conversion, but the Initiative's gathering of diverse Catholics together in conversation and worship is itself a sign of grace.

And, yet, the Initiative has not fulfilled the somewhat unrealistic expectations placed on it by others at its founding. The early death of Cardinal Bernardin, for instance, deprived the Initiative of the kind of visibility and influence in the church that only a cardinal—and a holy, well-respected one at that—can provide. It has been difficult to find sufficient numbers of "conservative" or "orthodox" Catholics willing to participate in its activities. Minority and younger Catholics have also been underrepresented, though not for a lack of effort on the Initiative's part.

In his 2004 annual lecture, the *National Catholic Reporter*'s Vatican correspondent, John Allen, asked the pointed question, "Why didn't Common Ground work?" While fully supporting the aims of the Initiative, he also noted that it hadn't had its desired impact and that polarization actually seemed to have intensified in the years since its founding. The problem, he suggested, was perhaps the lack of a "bottoming out" experience among many American Catholics: "They have not had the kind of illumination, the 'ah-ha' moment, in which they grasped the sterility of ideological warfare. . . . In some fashion, however, Catholics need to be brought to see how their blinders and prejudices, far from safeguarding the faith, actually impede full Catholicity."

Moreover, Allen noted that matters of identity, rather than of dialogue, seemed to be the "strongest single impulse in the Christian community" throughout the world, particularly among many younger Catholics. The battles that have afflicted Catholicism for the past forty years, especially since the ecclesial and cultural traumas of 1968, are often unknown or regarded—rightly or not—as irrelevant or minor by such Catholics. They will not be attracted to a project that seems to water down their commitments and beliefs, and so Allen said that any spirituality or practice of dialogue will have to build upon "a vigorous assertion of identity, opening up our distinctive language and rituals and worldview to those who hunger for them." Many participants at the 2004 Cardinal Bernardin Conference on the wisdom of Catholic sexual teaching, for example, were struck by the desire of a number of the younger Catholics present to emphasize the life-giving dimensions of that teaching, even on such matters as birth control, which seemed passé or repellent to some older Catholics. That particular conference, for all of its limits, had the merit of showing that dialogue and a strong sense of identity can—even if with some difficulty—be mutually reinforcing. If the Initiative is to have a lasting impact on the church, then, it will need to continue to underscore the urgency of its work and find ways to attract younger Catholics to that work.

The Scope and Structure of This Book

Much has changed in the church and in the world in the short time since the conference on the priesthood in 2003. Most dramatically, the death of Pope John Paul II and the election of Cardinal Joseph Ratzinger as Pope Benedict XVI in April 2005 have brought Catholicism into a new phase of its history. The clerical sexual-abuse crisis, while in some ways less acute now than in 2002, continues to wound the church and sap its energy for mission; financial and institutional aftershocks, such as diocesan reconfigurations and declarations of bankruptcy, continue to reverberate. The American-led war in Iraq began on March 20, 2003—just weeks after the conference—and continues still with little end in sight. The 2004 presidential election between George Bush and John Kerry highlighted the ongoing polarization that plagues national politics and culture.

The fundamental themes and questions raised by the conference, however, remain as pressing as ever. This book thus aims, first, to present the main topics and concerns that emerged at the conference and, second, to use them as a springboard for reflection on the priesthood's present and future. Accordingly, I have woven together comments of the conference participants, contributions from other ecclesial and theological voices, and my own analyses. At every point, I have tried carefully to distinguish and to relate these diverse voices.

This book is not an official statement of the Initiative—nor could it be, as conference participants and the members of the Initiative's advisory committee hold a range of positions—but it does seek to further its goals: seeking common ground rooted in scripture and tradition, identifying differences respectfully and constructively, building up the friendship and trust necessary for genuine ecclesial communion. It will be more illustrative than exhaustive in its treatment of various topics. I do not claim, for example, the sociological expertise of Dean Hoge's and Jacqueline Wenger's *Evolving Visions of the Priesthood* or Andrew Greeley's *Priests: A Calling in Crisis*, but I do draw extensively on those works. I offer signposts, rather than a definitive, last word.

The first chapter examines the cultural and ecclesial contexts of the priesthood in today's church; themes of change and darkness characterized this discussion at the conference. The next three chapters examine the priest as a "man of communion," to borrow a phrase from Pope John Paul II's document on priestly formation (*Pastores dabo vobis*, 18). The second chapter explores the priest's communion with Christ. How, in the light of Christ who is the foundation and goal of his life and ministry, does the priest see himself as disciple and as minister? The third chapter takes up the priest's communion with his bishop and with other priests. The fourth chapter addresses the priest's communion with the laity and with himself. How, for instance, ought the priest relate to a laity increasingly aware of its "adulthood"? How do his experiences of intimacy and sexuality shape his identity and ministry? I end with a conclusion outlining some common themes and areas of agreement from the conference, as well as offering points for future reflection on a priesthood that has been "tested in every way."

Acknowledgments and Dedication

Even a book as brief as this one puts its author in the grateful debt of many people. The Catholic Common Ground Initiative graciously extended the invitation to write this book. I learned much from the conference participants and hope that I have done justice to their contributions. Catherine Patten, R.S.H.M., the Initiative's coordinator, has been a patient supporter and a generous conversation partner. Father Robert Imbelli, Monsignor Dennis Sheehan, and Monsignor John Strynkowski applied to the manuscript the theological insight and pastoral wisdom gained from their collective 125 years of priestly ministry. Nicholas Zinos transcribed with care the conference proceedings. John Jones, editorial director of the Crossroad Publishing Company, brought this book to life through his hard work and unfailing wit. And, finally, I thank my wife, Deborah, and our two boys, Peter and Luke, for making my writing possible through their gifts of time and love.

This book is dedicated to two priests, Cardinal Joseph Bernardin and Monsignor Philip Murnion. Although they had markedly different personalities—the cardinal was reserved and marked by a Southern graciousness; Phil was effusive and a New Yorker to his restless core—each spent his life in the service of Christ and his church, and each had a gift for bringing and keeping people together. Both knew suffering deeply, as each lost his father at an early age, and each was afflicted with terminal cancer—the cardinal in his pancreas, Phil in his colon. Cardinal Bernardin, of course, suffered the further indignity of a false accusation of sexual abuse. And, most important, both died with uncommon grace and transparency to the Lord, befitting priests who daily celebrated his paschal mystery.

In his address in October 1996 to the first meeting of the Initiative's advisory committee—his last major speech before his death the following month—the cardinal drew on his experience of suffering to call one last time for reconciliation in the church:

> A dying person does not have time for the peripheral or the accidental. He or she is drawn to the essential, the important—yes, the eternal. And what is important, my friends, is that we find that unity with the Lord and within the community of faith for which

Jesus prayed so fervently on the night before he died. To say it quite boldly, it is wrong to waste the precious gift of time given to us, as God's chosen servants, on acrimony and division.

We are still far from realizing the urgency of the cardinal's— and Jesus'—call to common ground. I hope that this book will in some small way respond to that call, and I gratefully dedicate these reflections on the priesthood to Joseph Bernardin and Philip Murnion, priests of Christ, the great high priest.

Chapter One

The Cultural and Ecclesial Contexts of Catholic Priesthood Today

The first day of the conference was devoted to the contemporary contexts and experiences of priests. Four papers—by Scott Appleby, Gerald Fogarty, Dean Hoge, and Susan Wood—formed the starting point for discussion. Discussion of Fogarty's paper on the historical relationship in the United States between priests and bishops will be held for chapter 3, where that relationship is examined in greater detail. So, too, will the conversation prompted by Hoge's and Wood's papers be taken up in subsequent chapters, which address the sociological and theological factors that shape priests' relationships with other members of the church.

Cultural Contexts

The historian Scott Appleby, from the University of Notre Dame, was asked by the conference organizers to "anticipate features of the world in which tomorrow's priests will be ministering." Limiting itself to those priests who would be ordained in the next decade or so in the United States, his paper, "Defending 'Truth,' Negotiating Pluralism, Evoking

Hope: Once and Future Challenges to the Priesthood," outlined three challenges and three tasks facing the church and its priests. First is the challenge of "popular skepticism." Skepticism, literally "consideration" or "doubt," has taken many forms throughout history, but at its core is doubt about reason's ability to come to "reliable conclusions about the ultimate nature of reality." Existing since antiquity, it nonetheless has taken on particularly sharp form in recent decades. Appleby notes the rise of nonfoundationalism, which denies even the possibility of universal and discernible foundations for knowledge, and its cultural counterpart in a distorted multiculturalism that rejects universal truths and promotes hyperindividualism. These philosophical and cultural movements have led to a profound crisis of reason and the spread of moral relativism. "Agnosticism about the underlying meaning of human life," he writes, "has been elevated to the level of a working assumption in the everyday lives of a significant and growing minority of Americans."

Still more devastating than such agnosticism, though, is the rise of what the Canadian philosopher Charles Taylor has called "melancholy." In previous generations, melancholy was felt as meaninglessness, as alienation from a fixed, objective framework of being and meaning. Today, however, that guarantee of meaning, that independent existence of God or some other framework of meaning, has disappeared. Melancholy, as Taylor describes it, is no longer alienation or exile but emptiness: the deepest truth about reality may be its ultimate nothingness. This specter of nihilism, Appleby writes, touches all generations: senior citizens who recall the Holocaust and the Gulag; Boomers who have experienced the "death of God," Vietnam, and the "degradation of political idealism along a slope dug by Nixon and paved by Clinton"; Gen Xers living through unprecedented family breakdown, AIDS, and declining economic prospects. Far from being an esoteric, abstract problem, then, the crisis of skepticism has profound effects on the cultures and the churches in which priests minister.

Appleby identifies the second challenge facing the church as the erosion of biblical and theological literacy. The rise of popular skepticism contributes not only to a pervasive melancholy but also to a hermeneutic of suspicion that is hostile to authority and to such authorities' desire to construct grand narratives of, say, "progress" or "redemption." These overarching narratives are held to twist reality by obscuring or even erasing marginalized groups from history; they also present history as a purportedly orderly, linear process, when it is actually directionless and random. This collapse under the weight of suspicion of universal and all-encompassing worldviews reaches into the Christian churches. The erosion of a biblical worldview—the easy, familiar reference to someone as a Judas or a Martha, the shared language and vision of covenant and common good—leads to an impoverishment of the churches' and the nation's imagination. The scriptural language and images that contributed so much, for instance, to American civil rights and social justice movements have largely disappeared, without any sufficiently "thick" replacements; individualism and utilitarianism, the "regnant American idioms," are incapable of inspiring social transformation. In addition, among Catholics of European origin this biblical erosion has been complemented by the disappearance of the neighborhoods and ghettos that fostered a web of belief, devotion, worship, and authority. For Catholicism, a sacramental religion in which identity is transmitted primarily through ritual, biblical, and sacramental illiteracy is doubly wounding. And, I would add, such illiteracy and fragmentation make the work of preaching and presiding all the more difficult for priests.

This erosion of literacy combines with the rise of popular skepticism to produce a third challenge, which Appleby calls a "fractious pluralism that undermines the possibility of a genuinely diverse but unified moral and religious community." While affirming that diversity and pluralism are often valuable, even necessary goods, he warns that the increasingly fractured nature of social and ecclesial life often leads to new forms of tribalism, in which group identity is defined over against another group or individual. Such tribalism often takes the form of religious fundamentalism that seeks to "shore up religious authority and truth" through recourse to a "selective retrieval" of religious traditions and texts, appeals to inerrancy and infallibility, and the demonization of one's opponents as insufficiently pure or orthodox. Appleby notes that in Catholicism the trend to enclaves spans the ideological spectrum. He mentions, among others, expressions of Catholic feminism that separate themselves from parochial and diocesan life, and I would add the increasingly virulent attacks by some in the Catholic Right against church leaders on Internet blogs and other media. The irony, of course, is that such sectarianism and solipsism are perfect expressions of the very individualism and postmodernism so contested by fundamentalists of all stripes. I think here of the truth that one often becomes what one hates.

And, for an American church whose growth and future will come largely from immigrants from Latin America and Asia, the changing shape of immigration poses new opportunities and dangers to national and ecclesial unity. Television, e-mail, inexpensive telecommunications, and air travel all permit unprecedented connectedness to countries of origin. But, they can also enable a resistance to integration (not co-optation) into American society, a fragmentation of a unified national identity. So, too, will the future of Catholicism in America depend on the ability of its members and leaders to both welcome the diverse gifts of immigrants and integrate such believers into the broader community, in order that these gifts build up the church. Catholic life and ministry in coming decades will be successful, then, to the extent that they are hospitable and collaborative.

Faced with these three challenges, which Appleby notes are not exhaustive, American priests are called to, first, model catholicity in the face of pluralism; second, defend objective truth over against rootlessness and skepticism; and, third, speak about the obstacles to hope.

Appleby's paper launched a wide-ranging discussion on the cultural contexts of the contemporary priesthood. While the conversation was at times intensely intellectual (mostly a positive thing), it also drew upon the experiences of the conference participants. Cletus Kiley, the then-executive director of the USCCB's Secretariat for Priestly Life and Ministry and present president and C.E.O. of The Faith and Politics Institute, said that the hermeneutic of suspicion has spread throughout the church and presbyterates as a result of the sexual-abuse crisis: "People begin to wonder, 'Where did this [priest or bishop] come from? How did we get him?' . . . I suspect any kind of person who is in a leadership role, in a hierarchical role, is a target of that hermeneutic of suspicion." Monsignor Francis Kelley, pastor of Sacred Heart Parish in Roslindale, Massachusetts, noted:

In many ways the priesthood finds itself in the middle of the darkness and doesn't even know it. The serious reaction among clergy, at least in Boston, involves three things. There is serious depression, and enormous shame, and a growing anger. Those are the emotional activities going on among the presbyterate in Boston, and many people want to deny all three. Some will say they're there, and some others acknowledge they're there.... There's a sense of "Can we really take the darkness seriously?" That's not something we want to do, but I don't think we have much choice.... When it's out of the public eye, then complacency sets in again. And I fear that's where we're going.

Another Boston priest, Monsignor Dennis Sheehan, senior chaplain at the Harvard Catholic Chaplaincy and the pastor of St. Paul's Parish in Cambridge, said that the most problematic divide in the church is not between progressives and traditionalists but between the grassroots and the leadership, between the parish and the bishop; too often a large gap exists in bishops' and parishes' (and their pastors') perceptions of one another; distrust and distance exacerbate each other. Sheehan suggested—with a mixture of jest and complete seriousness—that bishops and priests needed to go on a marriage encounter, in order to learn how to fight constructively—a skill that is not part of their formation or of clerical culture.

Underlying much of this suspicion, several participants held, is an unwillingness to confront differences. Whether due to learned patterns of fear or deference, or to the avoidance of public conflict, clergy and laity alike are often unwilling or unable to speak freely. They don't love or trust one another enough to risk conflict. Ernesto Cortés, the southwest regional director of the Chicago-based Industrial Areas Foundation, said that his experience as a community organizer has helped him to see the potentially constructive role of conflict:

> The kind of friendship that is called for is a public friendship. The word I like is *philia*. A fellow named Herbert McCabe wrote a book called *God Still Matters*, and one of the things that he wrote in an essay is that Christ is always misunderstood and the church, like Christ, is at its best when it is always being misunderstood. So he argues that it has a public and a political role to play, but it is not the politics of the Democratic, Republican, or Labour Party. It's a different kind of political engagement which requires this concept of *philia*. Which means the kind of friendship which emerges among people who fight together, struggle together, disagree with each other, but always recognize that they've got to be there for one another, they've got to be in solidarity with one another and back each other up. . . . One of the reasons why we can't form good friendships with people we work with is that we don't know how to fight with them very well. And I think we have to learn how to teach people how to use conflict as a way of deepening a relationship. In my work, the people that I work the best with and have the best collegial relationship with—the other organizers—are people I have fought with like cats and dogs. And we use those fights to deepen

our understanding of where we come from, our stories, our backgrounds, our situations, our way of looking at one another.

These perceptions of suspicion and alienation exemplified the climate of "darkness" to which so many participants referred throughout the conference. The clerical sexual-abuse crisis was, of course, the dominant point of reference, but the conference as a whole agreed that the darkness predated the crisis and was larger than it. Nor, it should be added, did anyone suggest that such darkness was a "liberal" or "conservative" problem. Patricia Kelly, a psychologist who works extensively with church communities, summarized the dilemma:

> I was quite caught yesterday about how many times the darkness would come up, and then, in true Catholic fashion, somebody would rescue us and say "No, no, no, no. It's really not that dark. It's really not that bleak. We're really doing a great job and things are okay." I can't tell you the number of meetings I've gone to in all kinds of Catholic life, where people get close to a problem and they are almost ready to name the problem—to use Frank Kelley's language, "to name the lie"—and then the anxiety of the unknown, the habit of so many of us who came from families where "Be nice and keep your mouth shut" was sort of the ordinary way of being, takes over. We normalize it, we go back, we pat one another on the shoulder, we offer one another a cup of coffee or pizza, we affirm each other about how good we really are despite the

limited resources we have, and the problem remains—safe and toxic and growing.

So, let me name the darkness. I believe the darkness is a gift from God, and I believe that the darkness is a place of great mercy and great hope. But if it is a source of hope that we need it to be, we're going to need to embrace and look at our own skepticism, our own cultural skepticism, that allows us to be so conflict-avoidant, that allows us to normalize competitiveness, jealousy, gossip. We need to look at our fear of failure, our fear of rejection, our fear of change, and, most importantly, our fear of being known.

. . . Whatever that darkness is, in the absence of embracing it, we are perpetrators of the violence that separates us from the Redemption and separates us from grace. So I would say that, to be men and women of the Word, to be men and women who are willing to labor, to give birth, not knowing what that birth may mean, we need to be able to embrace the darkness, to name problems, to call ourselves to accountability, to be unafraid, and to believe that if the church is what it says it is, it—despite our best efforts and despite our lack of belief—simply cannot fail.

Several participants pressed the "darkness discussion" into explicitly theological dimensions. Robert Imbelli, a priest of the New York archdiocese who teaches theology at Boston College, said:

Part of the difficulty is that we have very cheap talk about salvation: "Jesus saves," "Is Jesus your savior?"

And I think the problem with that is we don't take into account what we are saved from. And this gets us back to the whole darkness motif that has taken up part of the day. Are we willing to come to grips with the darkness? Because unless we come to grips with our deep need to be saved, then salvation is always going to be cheap. . . . Speaking theologically, there's been a whole liberal Protestant trend over the past century which I think has now taken root in the Catholic Church, in which original sin is seen as some sort of vestige of a medieval benightedness. And so there is this unwillingness to face the darkness.

Monsignor John Strynkowski, the then-executive director of the USCCB's Secretariat for Doctrine and Pastoral Practices and current rector of St. James Cathedral–Basilica in Brooklyn, agreed with much of Imbelli's analysis but questioned whether American culture was as devoid of a sense of sin as some participants (and public commentators) had argued:

Being a New Yorker, I hope you will excuse my provincialism, but I maintain that the *New York Times Sunday Book Review* is the great record of sin in our time. When you read the book reviews of novels and of books of history, what you read is the failure of conscience, the failure of adherence to moral principles. I don't think our culture is totally bleak in terms of a sense of sin. And there are novelists, I think, who are portraying that, and maybe there are openings in the culture that can help us bring our own message of salvation.

For his part, Paul Griffiths, the Schmitt Professor of Catholic Studies at the University of Illinois–Chicago, argued that such emphasis on darkness could be overstated:

> A fundamental Christian assumption is that we are all each of us fundamentally, structurally disordered. 1 Timothy 1:15, as you all remember, reads: "So this is a truth worthy to be believed: Jesus Christ came into the world to save sinners." And here's the kicker, "Among whom I am the first." . . . It's a fundamental Christian confession for laypeople and priests alike. The surprise to me is not when Christians do dreadful things, the surprise to me is always rather when they don't. So I suppose it depends on one's starting point. This darkness that we face, the dreadful things that priests and laity have done, are doing, and will continue to do—it's just not surprising. It's in fact what human beings are like, even under the explicit relationship to the grace of Christ. So I'd rather we weren't sort of mysterious about darkness. It's not that mysterious. It's just what we're like.

These exchanges reflect, I think, a much broader conversation in the church. At the 2005 Synod of Bishops, for instance, a number of participants lamented the loss of a sense of sin, particularly in Western cultures. The church's teaching on the sacraments of Eucharist and reconciliation, they held, is emptied out when believers and nonbelievers alike do not acknowledge the reality of sin. As a teacher of undergraduates at a Catholic institution, I sympathize with this critique. My students are much more comfortable with the language of "mistakes" and "errors" and "problems." "Sin" rarely crosses their lips, and they usually find talk of "salvation" and "redemption" to be nearly meaningless. Most, too, have drunk deeply of what the sociologist Alan Wolfe has called "moral freedom"— the sense that one must decide for oneself what is moral; "higher authority," he puts it, "has to tailor its commandments to the needs of real people." They find it hard to grasp that, sometimes, it is they—and not the church—who must change.

I think, though, that many of my students actually have a deep, if almost wholly unarticulated and inarticulate, sense of sin. They have experienced their parents' divorces, for instance, and they've lived through the breakup of sexually active relationships. They know what it means to fail and to be failed. The real problem may be the lack of an adequate language to describe and to shape their experiences. And, here, the church surely bears a large measure of responsibility for failing to form its members adequately in its distinctive ways of speaking and living. I think that such leaders as Timothy Radcliffe and Cardinal Francis George are right in arguing that the deeper issue is not primarily the loss of a sense of sin, but of losing sight of the breadth and depth of God's love for humanity. Radcliffe speaks of an "unbearable sense of guilt" that plagues so many in the absence of knowing that they are loved "in all [their] weakness" by God.[1] Cardinal George says that many Americans lack an awareness that forgiveness and a truly new beginning are possible. He argues that in American culture, like the modern West in general, "everything is permitted, but nothing is forgiven," because the dominant culture is built on the control of self and nature to such an extent that "anything that is unintended is an affront." The church, in this situation, is to show the world that "there is much activity that is forbidden. But in the end everything can be forgiven."[2] Love allows for a new beginning. In light of this, I suggest that the darkness furthered by the sexual-abuse crisis creates an opportunity to encounter again the reality of Christian love. And, the loss of a sense of sin may actually reveal how both the church and the world have banalized God's love: if God's love is cheap and saccharine, then so too will one's sense of sin be cheap and saccharine. The priest's task in this environment might be not so much to lament a sick culture as to invite it to an encounter with Christ's healing, demanding love—a love that led him to the cross.

Apart from the discussion on darkness, one of the more fruitful points raised during the conference was the irony that American Catholics are the best-educated laity in the history of Catholicism and yet betray a surprising ignorance of, or illiteracy in, their faith. Frank Kelley noted, for instance, that some priests find it easier to deal with immigrant parishioners, who often lack much formal education, than with more educated, upper-middle-class ones. In Boston, such "educated" believers form the backbone of movements like Voice of the Faithful. Other conference participants noted, though, that even the best-educated and professionally successful Catholics are often woefully unformed in their beliefs. Gerald Fogarty, a Jesuit church historian who teaches at the University of Virginia, gave a striking example:

> A young man I know came to me. He's a neurosurgical resident. He has a Ph.D. and an M.D., and he finished both of them before he was thirty. He was looking for spiritual direction, and I suggested some Augustine, and he said, "I've never heard of him." Yet

the average priest I know is intimidated by the fact that his parishioners are far better educated, and [yet] they are not well-trained in religion.

Fogarty called for priests to be more active in the education and formation of their people, and to have greater confidence in that work.

A number of participants also noted the relative lack of attention in the preparatory papers to minority Catholics (roughly 20 percent of the participants, however, were minorities). Hispanic concerns in particular came to the forefront, befitting a conference held in San Antonio. Taking up a theme raised in Scott Appleby's paper, David García, rector of San Fernando Cathedral in San Antonio, said that Mexican-Americans, unlike European-Americans, have always returned and crossed back to the mother country; they thus offer to the church in the United States a model of how identity and difference can hold together. Roberto Piña, the former director of the USCCB's Southwest Office of Hispanic Affairs and a founder of the Worldwide Marriage Encounter movement in Spanish, spoke of his frustrations at the treatment Hispanic Catholics sometimes received in the past—"they were placed where their liturgy had to be in the basement, there were moments when they were criticized because they smelled, they were farm workers"—but also of his gratitude for those priests who studied Spanish and learned about Hispanic cultures. Ultimately, he concluded, "we really don't care how much you know, but what we really want to know is how much you care—when you recognize our little kids, when you touch them on the face." Neil Connolly, pastor of St. Mary's Church on Manhattan's Lower East Side, drew on over forty years of ministry with Hispanic communities in saying that it is important for priests to share the lifestyles of the people they serve:

> I went to a lecture a long time ago when I first went to Puerto Rico to study language and before being assigned to a Spanish parish. I remember the speaker talking about kenosis, talking about poverty, about becoming one with the people, learning their customs, learning their way of life. I think it raises a lot of questions about the way we live in terms of poverty, lifestyle, what we give up. Sometimes the professional appearance can very much get in the way of the approachability with people. And I used to get very tired at priests' funerals, although I understand the hyperbole that's very often used about Monsignor-so-and-so, when, you know, [it was said that] he was the one who really raised this parish, and none of the people are ever mentioned in the same sentence.

Donald Wolf, a past president of the National Federation of Priests' Councils who has served as vicar for Hispanic ministry in the Oklahoma City archdiocese, suggested that where North Americans think of the world as perfectible and so emphasize problem solving, Hispanic Catholics tend to see the world as redeemable and so can be more accepting of the limits of human activity. These differences naturally give rise to varying conceptions and models of ecclesial life and ministry, which we will explore in subsequent chapters.

Amidst this broad range of cultural and ecclesial contexts, I was struck by the absence from the conversation of the perspectives of young Catholics (defined broadly as those under forty). While this oversight was likely due to the paucity of such younger voices—only three of the nearly fifty participants were under forty years old, none were under thirty, only one priest was under forty-five years old, and no seminarians of any age were present—it nonetheless hindered discussion on generational differences in the priesthood and in individual dioceses and religious communities. I would have liked to have heard from younger seminarians and priests about the origins of their vocations, their hopes for ministry and for the church, and their relationships with the laity and with priests and seminary faculty.

So, too, would it have helped to have looked more closely at the younger Catholics to whom priests of all ages and perspectives will minister in the years to come. Co-authored by Mary Johnson, S.N.D. de N., a member of the Initiative's advisory committee, *Young Adult Catholics: Religion in the Culture of Choice*, for instance, offers a fascinating statistical and interpretative account of such believers. Positively, they like being Catholic and have little desire to join another church or religion; they are also strongly attached to key Catholic beliefs and practices such as the sacraments, Christ's real presence in the Eucharist, service to the poor, and devotion to Mary. Negatively, they can be individualistic and have problems with commitment; where the alienation from the church of some Baby-Boomer Catholics is dependent on a prior sense of attachment, younger Catholics are often simply indifferent toward the church: they are not as angry, because they're not as attached. Catholicism is less central to their personal identity, and so as a whole they are less invested in the future of the church as a visible, structured community. And, for all of their attraction to the sacraments, their sacramental practice is

weak. Their high levels of belief in central doctrines are necessary but not sufficient for maintaining a vibrant Catholic
identity, and, in the absence of a greater sacramental practice
and coherent religious identity, these "communal" or "cultural" Catholics will wither away. "The demise of a religious
tradition is not about the death of the old, but the failure to
retain the young," the authors of *Young Adult Catholics* conclude, and thus they contend that the most pressing task in a
"culture of choice" will be to articulate and foster a distinctive
Catholic identity that focuses on discipleship, community,
and the sacraments.[3]

The conference papers and conversation sketched a broad,
if not definitive, portrait of the contemporary contexts of the
priesthood in the United States. As I reflect on that conversation, two contrasting voices who weren't present at the conference keep drawing my attention: Cardinal Francis George
and Andrew Greeley. The Chicagoans are friends and offer a
provocative counterpoint in their evaluation of the church's
relationship with American culture, and the implications of
that relationship for priestly life and ministry.

Cardinal George, particularly since his installation as
archbishop of Chicago in 1997, has drawn a sharp contrast
between the cultures of Catholicism and of the United States.
He tells a story of the differences between Pope John Paul II's
visits to St. Louis and Mexico City in 1999. In Mexico City,
the pope's motorcade was greeted on streets lined with thou-
sands of people held back only by a human chain of youth
with joined hands. Many of these same youth provided security and hospitality for the visiting bishops, and few police
officers were visible during the visit. The overall effect, the
cardinal says, "was not just a series of orchestrated events but a

public celebration in which the city itself participated." The St. Louis visit was successful, too, but marked by a level of security that kept the pope and the people at a distance: the Secret Service closed bridges, blocked off streets in the city center, prohibited parking. "Everything," he writes, "was secure; but contact, human relationship, was kept to a minimum."

While mindful of the need to ensure the pope's safety, he wonders whether the two visits revealed a contrast between a Mexican, Catholic culture of relationship and communion and an American, Protestant one of autonomy and control. Above all, he suggests that "in the United States today relationships are suspect because they threaten control." Americans suffer from a "poverty of imagination" that limits human interactions to commercial and legal contracts and so keeps them from seeing relationships as liberating.[4] This "secularized Puritanism" of much American culture, in his view, sees God as the greatest threat to human freedom and thus strips him of power. Instead of "killing" God, as Nietzsche proposed, American secularism "tames" God so that he cannot influence the world. God is reduced to a projection of human desires and no longer makes demands on us. Because this "God" no longer has any power, the church, too, loses its divine authority to call people to conversion and devolves into a club whose membership is based on affinity rather than conversion. Religion becomes a privatized hobby, a "leisure-time activity, not a way of life." So long as the church accepts this domestication of its God and its mission, then secular culture is content to let it be. When the church rejects it, however, the culture actively threatens it: politically, legally, economically, journalistically.[5] Moreover, the church finds itself attacked not only from without, but also from within: the Catholic Left rejects its sexual and ecclesiological teaching, and the Catholic Right criticizes those bishops it deems to be insufficiently orthodox.[6]

These secular and ecclesial cultural conditions have contributed, in the cardinal's judgment, to the greatest failure of the postconciliar church: its failure to form a laity capable of engaging and transforming the world in the light of the gospel.[7] The church, in this situation, must reacknowledge the power and authority of God that come through the bishops and recommit itself to forming disciples who by their alternative way of life manifest true freedom. This witness to freedom will make the church's mission to American culture one of healing and fulfillment: the healing of its individualism and the fulfillment of its founding vision of liberty in a diverse unity.[8] This mission necessarily places great demands on the church and its priests.

The priest-sociologist Andrew Greeley, like Cardinal George, holds up a distinctively Catholic vision of reality—what he calls the "Catholic imagination," which sees grace lurking in all of creation—and is unafraid to criticize those who water down the Catholic heritage or reduce religion to morality or doctrinal adherence. Unlike George, though, Greeley spends little time criticizing American culture (except for what he claims is its inherent anti-Catholicism, as "American as cherry pie"). The church's primary enemies and problems are not external ones such as materialism and relativism, but internal ones: "stupidity, incompetence, and clerical culture," as he writes with characteristic understatement.[9]

In *The Catholic Revolution: New Wine, Old Wineskins, and the Second Vatican Council*, he argues that the "new wine" of Vatican II—a sense that the seemingly changeless church could and did change—caused the "old wineskins" of nineteenth-century structures and mindsets to burst; even moderate change proved too much for the old forms to bear.[10] Tensions that had built up in the church's defensive reaction to the Enlightenment and the French Revolution rushed forward uncontrollably and destroyed a rule-driven Catholicism that was strong but brittle.

Particularly in the wake of *Humanae vitae* (1968), a split arose between the higher clergy (the pope, cardinals, and other bishops), on the one hand, and the lower clergy and the laity, on the other. Priests and the laity decided, rightly or wrongly, that if the council had changed some aspects of the church, then others were open to revision. They would henceforth be Catholics on their own terms—a development that Greeley as a sociologist neither endorses nor condemns but simply reports.

In the aftermath of this revolution, some tried to restore the old wineskins; others tried to deny or didn't realize that Vatican II was "new wine"; still others tried to create new, idiosyncratic wineskins. All three attempts failed. Restoration simply responded to the crisis of authority with more authority; denial and obliviousness met with predictable results, and much modernization issued forth in what yet another Chicago priest, Robert Barron, has called "Beige Catholicism": an often elitist religion cobbled together by "progressive" liturgists and theologians that was shorn of Catholicism's historical beauty, poetry, and distinctiveness. Greeley is particularly critical of liturgical "experts," who stripped church sanctuaries and walls of their art and banished popular devotions.

Greeley argues that the way forward will involve a much-overdue admission by church leadership that the radical change wrought by the Catholic revolution was caused in part by the preconciliar church's suppression of even modest, necessary reforms. Leadership will also have to admit that Vatican II did in fact make substantial changes in the life of the church; the council was not merely an "occurrence" of clarification and continuity but an "event" of transformation and even discontinuity. Renewal will involve, too, the adoption of a vastly different style of leadership and formation. The aforementioned "stupidity, incompetence, and clerical culture" must be overcome. In their place must be a vision of leadership as charm that presents the beauty of the faith and invites people to an ongoing experience of that beauty; adult, educated Catholics will not respond to commands but instead must be listened to and respected as equals—however frustrating that may be to leaders desirous of obedience. There must also be a renewed commitment to formation in the Catholic imagination—that "rainforest" of ritual, beauty, myth, and worship that keeps Catholics Catholic in the face of their frustrations with the church. "Attraction," Greeley writes, is the "only effective long-term strategy."

I find much in both George's and Greeley's approaches to be appealing and even complementary. If the cardinal's contrast of Catholicism and American culture is somewhat reductive in its generalizations, he nonetheless makes important points on the cultural and ecclesial hurdles the church faces in its mission. While I am skeptical of most litanies of complaint, it remains true that naming one's problems is essential to resolving them. Like the proverbial frog in a pot who doesn't realize that the increasingly hot water will soon boil it to death, many in the church fail to recognize or admit that the church faces enemies who do actively seek its destruction—whether through outright defeat or the more subtle control of "taming." One participant at the San Antonio conference, for example, reported a remark by a representative of Planned Parenthood who made clear that organization's desire to remove the Catholic Church from the American health-care system. I also appreciate George's confidence in Catholicism's ability to transform American culture, as well as his rejection of the term "counter-cultural" as insufficiently loving of the culture that is to be renewed. He is right in noting that the world is "both friendly and unfriendly, both holy and demonic," and that the church's mission must be to discern the legitimate demands and needs of the world, while challenging its distortions and traps. The world's transformation is possible only through what he calls a "disinterested" rather than "possessive" love on the church's part.

And, if Greeley seems to romanticize—as perhaps only a clerical critic of clericalism can—the goodness and long-sufferingness of the American Catholic laity, his affirmation of a distinctive Catholic identity has the rare merit of being both unembarrassed and nontriumphalistic. In particular, his emphasis on beauty as the best possible means of catechesis and mission is dead-on. Unfortunately, so, too, is his claim that American Catholicism—especially its leadership—places virtually no value on it. Without such beauty, the church's "truth" will devolve into fundamentalism and its "goodness" into a rigorist moralism.[11] Furthermore, his appreciation of beauty combines with an empirical sensitivity to keep him from easy recourse to "isms" of all stripes: consumerism, fundamentalism, individualism, relativism, and so on. These terms have a real, but limited, efficacy and often serve to foster intellectual and pastoral laziness, even despair. Greeley rightly notes that blaming the "culture" and its ills often degenerates into an excuse for a lack of pastoral imagination and effort on the part of church leaders.

While I believe that George's and Greeley's readings of the relationship between church and culture are largely complementary, even in their markedly different approaches, it seems that their most significant difference—one especially pertinent for any consideration of the contemporary priesthood—concerns the nature of Christian life in the church. Put perhaps too simply, Greeley emphasizes the "big tent" of belonging, and George the "narrow way" of discipleship. Greeley glories in creation and incarnation, discerning God's grace lurking everywhere and in everyone—even, perhaps, in clerical culture. George rejoices in the cross and resurrection; grace is abundant and free, but exacting. The two emphases are not exclusive—Greeley would certainly not deny the gospel's demands, nor George the church's essential openness and hospitality—but a pastoral tension exists between generous invitation and demanding response.

Such tension is, of course, the perennial drama of Christian life, but it takes on an acute form in our time, especially in regard to priests, who by their very identity as disciples and ministers are called to build up Christian communities. Greeley, I judge, understands better what draws people into the church and leads them to return: the allure of beauty, the kindling of imagination through story and sacrament. He grasps, too, that the church's crisis of authority will be resolved only through renewed efforts of persuasion; imposition and repeated calls for obedience are generally not worthy of adults. George, however, offers a more compelling vision of discipleship, of the gospel's call to conversion and self-sacrifice for the sake of a greater joy. He seems more aware of the resistances in society and in hearts that shut out grace and create violence. The church, he insists, must move beyond the potentially vague sense of "belonging" that, at its worst, eviscerates the Christian life and reduces it to a lifestyle-option that precludes transformation in Christ; surely part of being an adult believer involves responding to challenges that can make us uncomfortable, challenges we'd rather not hear but that ultimately make us freer and more loving.

The priest's response to this tension between belonging and conversion—both in himself and in his people—shapes his entire ministry, and it is one to which we will return in this book. But, lest our reflections sink into hopeless abstraction, it will be helpful to turn to the sociological data on the priesthood presented at the conference.

Sociological Context

Dean Hoge, a sociologist at the Catholic University of America, prepared for the conference the paper "Characteristics of Priests in 2001,"[12] based on a survey of nearly 1,300 priests and personal interviews with twenty-seven priests. His findings were both sobering and hopeful. Most problematic is the aging and shrinking of the American presbyterate. In 2001: the average age of all priests was sixty, while that of active priests alone was fifty-six.

- Only 4 percent of priests were thirty-five or younger (compared to 22 percent in 1970), while 30 percent were seventy or older (compared to less than 7 percent in 1970).

- In the last thirty years the percentage of priests who are retired has risen from 3 percent to 16 percent.

Hoge's subsequent research has confirmed these trends:

- The average age of the newly ordained has risen from 27 in 1970, to 35 in 1998, and to 37.3 in 2005.
- The number of annual ordinations in recent years has varied between 440 and 540, which translates into a 35 percent to 45 percent replacement rate (the number of new priests needed to offset losses through death and resignation).
- Between 1985 and 2001 the total number of priests declined by 15 percent, while the total number of Catholics increased by 21 percent.[13]

Hoge's paper also noted the qualitative problems faced by priests. Although criticisms of seminary education have dropped significantly over the last three decades, priests still report significant dissatisfaction with the human and practical components of their formation; 59 percent agree, for instance, that "few attempts were made to help the seminarian learn how to deal with people." Older priests—particularly those between fifty-six and sixty-five—reported significant difficulties with "the way authority is exercised in the church," while younger priests especially noted "too much work" and "unrealistic demands and expectations of lay people." These last two complaints have nearly doubled since 1970—perhaps as a result of the priest shortage. Other common complaints were loneliness and "being expected to represent church teachings I have difficulty with." And, while priests reported that their strongest support came from "their families, non-priest friends, and staff members where they minister," they found less support from other priests and their bishops.

Nonetheless, in the midst of this statistical implosion, Hoge reports that average levels of priestly happiness have increased dramatically over the last thirty years, an increase due in large part to the increased morale of younger priests.

- 94 percent consider themselves "very" or "pretty" happy, a level of happiness that equals or exceeds that of the average American man with a college or graduate degree.
- 88 percent of priests say that they would choose the priesthood again (up from 78 percent in 1970).
- 79 percent say that they "definitely" will not leave (up from 59 percent in 1970); 95 percent, in fact, now report that they will "definitely" or "probably" not leave, while only 1 percent "probably" or "definitely" will leave.
- Only 12 percent of priests would "certainly" or "probably" pursue marriage if celibacy became optional (down from 18 percent in 1970).

Lastly, priests find their deepest satisfactions in celebrating the sacraments, preaching, and having the "opportunity to work with many people and be a part of their lives."

Although Hoge's research was conducted before the outbreak of the sexual-abuse crisis of 2002, subsequent, postcrisis studies have confirmed these findings. Drawing on the results of a *Los Angeles Times* survey in 2002 and other studies over the past three decades, Andrew Greeley argues that priests as a group remain happy and fulfilled in their ministry, celibacy, and personal lives. He notes in *Priests: A Calling in Crisis* that they report levels of satisfaction in their work that are significantly higher than other professionals such as physicians, lawyers, college professors, and Protestant clergy. Ninety-two percent would choose priesthood again (a higher rate than the proportion of married people who would choose the same spouse again). Moreover, 91 percent would encourage another man to enter the priesthood, whereas only half of physicians would similarly recommend their profession to young people today. Those who leave the priesthood do so not primarily because of celibacy, but because they are unhappy in their work.

The happiest priests, Greeley argues, are those "religious altruists" who find their greatest joys in "sacred" work such as preaching and presiding and their greatest challenges in "direct" ministerial matters such as evangelization, helping the poor, and keeping the church and the gospel relevant. Although only 7 percent of all priests, they are notably happier than those who find their deepest joy in "profane" tasks— "helping others and sharing in their lives"—and whose biggest challenges come from within (e.g., burnout, loneliness, lack of prayer) or without (e.g., the media, secularism, materialism, apathy). He is particularly critical of those who "complain about the world"[14] as the source of their greatest ministerial difficulties. The church's most dangerous enemies, he contends, are internal: its "incompetence, stupidity, and clerical culture" are far more troubling than the purported relativism and secularism of the surrounding culture.[15]

Greeley's greatest concern, though, is the substantial disconnect between the perceptions and evaluations that priests and laity have of each other. Seeing clericalism as the heart of the problem, he writes that priests are "surprisingly insensitive to their laity. Most priests dismiss them as lacking in faith, spirituality, and prayer life as well as being victims of apathy, materialism, secularism, and individualism." What is more troubling, he notes that very few priests even sense the laity's "massive dissatisf[action]" with their ministry.[16] Only 18 percent of Catholic laity, for instance, rate their priests' preaching as "excellent," compared to 36 percent of Protestant laity. Less than 30 percent of Catholic laity consider "excellent" their priests' respect for women, counseling abilities, youth work, or liturgical presiding. With typical bluntness, he concludes, "A quarter of the Catholic people think that their priests do a miserable job on almost all of their pastoral activities, and a sixth say that their priests are doing a fine job."[17] He finds further grounds for discontent in the emergence of younger priests who, on the whole, tend not to give much priority to lay ministry and insist on their distinctiveness over against such ministers and the laity in general. This last trend is particularly worrying, he claims, as the need for healthy laity–clergy collaboration will only increase in light of the rising number of lay ecclesial ministers and the declining numbers of priests.

Theological Context

Susan Wood, S.C.L., a professor of theology at Marquette University, in her essay, "The New Intra-ecclesial Context for an Understanding of Priesthood Today," joined theological reflection to an analysis of changing demographics and patterns of ministry in the contemporary church. She argued that any adequate theology of the priesthood must be contextual and relational. The priest and his ministry need to be seen in their contexts: the parish, the school, the mission, the chancery, the hospital, the city or suburb or countryside; a universal or "one-size-fits-all" theology is impossible. Demographic changes must also be taken into account: fewer priests overall, larger parishes, fewer residential pastors, increased numbers of lay ecclesial ministers. And, finally, these contextual and demographic changes affect the shape of priestly life and ministry itself: the priesthood is becoming increasingly "episcopal" and narrowly "cultic." As the size of parishes and the number of parishes assigned to each priest increase, priests increasingly assume roles of oversight (*episcopē*) and administration more proper to the bishop, while deacons increasingly assume many of the sacramental and pastoral responsibilities of priests. The priest's ministry is thus often reduced to sacramental dispensation that is largely separated from pastoral leadership. Priests risk being "divorced"—geographically and emotionally—from their people, a separation with predictable human and spiritual costs.

A theology of the priesthood must also be relational, viewing the priest in his communion with the other members of the church and with the world. Vatican II, according to Wood, made a decisive advance by describing all of the church's members—clergy, laity, and religious—through the paradigm of Christ's threefold office of priest, prophet, and king. In addition to developing a more adequate theology of baptism and of the universal call to holiness, this priest-prophet-king paradigm enabled a fuller theology of the priesthood. Where some previous models of priesthood focused sharply—even exclusively—on the priest as minister of the Eucharist and of reconciliation, the conciliar vision also encompassed preaching and pastoring. The council's terminology reflected this theological development, preferring "presbyter" to "priest." These conciliar developments indicated a move from an emphasis on sacred powers to one on pastoral leadership that embraces the prophetic and the priestly.

Building on this conciliar theology, Wood proposed that priestly identity be understood through a relational ontology. Sacramental ordination, in this view, is not primarily the conferral of sacred powers that elevate the priest above the laity, but a repositioning of the priest in relation to Christ and the church. It initiates the priest into a new relationship within the communion of the church. Just as baptism makes one a member of the church and confirmation a more public witness of that church, priestly ordination empowers one to act in a relationship of headship to the body of Christ. In this position of headship, the priest represents both Christ, the head of the church, and the entire body of believers. He acts *in persona Christi* and *in persona ecclesiae*. The priest's distinctiveness is found, paradoxically, only in his relatedness to the other members of the church:

> An ontology of relationship avoids the pitfalls of essentialism and functionalism. Not just anyone can perform a sacramental function because not everyone occupies the same relationship with respect to the Church. [And, a] danger of essentialism is that in insisting on the essential difference between priest and laity, we may forget the deep commonality between the laity and the priest in their common baptism. The two priesthoods—ministerial and

common—may be essentially different, but the priest
as a person is not essentially different from the rest of
the baptized because he shares baptismal identity
[with them].

A relational ontology also permits a more nuanced and
adequate understanding of the priest as an icon of Christ. This
image has become more prominent in recent years, particularly after the sexual-abuse crisis; and George Weigel—whom
Wood cited in her paper—is perhaps its most articulate and
effective expositor. In *The Courage to Be Catholic: Crisis,
Reform, and the Future of the Church*, he wrote that priests
should understand themselves not as "religious functionaries"
or as bureaucrats, but as "what the Catholic Church teaches
they are—living icons of the eternal priesthood of Jesus
Christ." Wood criticized this view on several grounds. She
noted the Cambridge historian Eamon Duffy's point that in
scholastic theology the representational or iconic dimension
of priesthood traditionally referred more to the priest's actions
than to his being. More importantly, many such "iconic" arguments diminish or neglect the iconicity that inheres in every
Christian through baptism; too often, she wrote, the language
of the priest as icon "absorb[s] baptismal identity into
ordained ministry identity." Vatican II, as a number of conference participants emphasized, avoided the language of the
priest as an *alter Christus*—"another Christ"—because all
Christians are "other Christs" through their baptism. Instead,
the council carefully described the priest as one who is config-
ured to and acts *in persona Christi capitis*—in the person of
Christ, the head. When this interplay of headship and baptismal equality is obscured or ignored, the danger arises of

separating the ordained priest from the priestly community that is the church; a head cannot exist without a body. Any adequate theology of the priesthood must therefore be thoroughly relational.

Christianity often speaks of such relationality through the language of communion—which comes from the Greek *koinōnia*, meaning "sharing" or "participation." The priest, as a "man of communion," in Pope John Paul II's fine phrase, receives his identity and his ministry from the communion he shares with Christ, his bishop or religious superior, his brother priests, his fellow baptized, and the entire human community. In the following chapters we will explore the nature of this manifold communion, beginning with the priest's relationship as disciple and minister of Christ, who is the origin and end of his Christian identity.

• Chapter Two •

The Priest in Relation to Christ

I think that believing people get a sense of whether a priest's life of prayer is or isn't characterized by this sort of steadiness, the long breaths for the long haul.... We can't uncover the face of Christ in people unless we have the habit of real attention to human faces in all their diversity—but also the habit of familiarity with the face of Christ. How do we recognize him, let alone help others to do so, if we are not spending time with that face, in the study of Scripture and adoration and silence? Faithful and persistent looking into the face of Jesus is the essential condition for connecting people with each other; without that, all we can offer is human goodwill, human shrinking from the cost of conflict, our own limited skills of sympathy and listening. But if we try to remain familiar with Jesus, we believe that our listening and mediating has a sacramental dimension, mostly imperceptible to us, but real and energizing. We are allowing some fuller reality in to the situation, the reality in whose climate we live: the priestly mediation of Christ.[1]

—Rowan Williams, Archbishop of Canterbury

Christianity, obvious as it may be to say, is personal. It is
not primarily about morals, institutions, or doctrines—
necessary though they are—but about a person, Jesus Christ,
who calls for a personal response. Neutrality and detachment
are not possible before him; we must engage him, risking our
identities and our lives. The key question, as Jesus poses it in
the Gospels to his disciples, is not "Who do people say that I
am?" but "Who do you say that I am?" The Christian life is
nothing other than the human response—intellectual, emotional, spiritual—to that question and that Person. It makes a
difference, then, whether we think of Jesus as primarily the
good shepherd, the teacher of the Beatitudes, the crucified
one, the healer, the friend, the prophet, to name only a few
central images. Our visions of Jesus shape, and are shaped by,
our visions of the church and its mission and ministry. It is no
surprise that social activists refer to Matthew 25 ("Whatever
you do to the least of these . . ."), for instance; prophets to
Luke 4 ("The Spirit of the Lord is upon me"); or evangelicals
to John 3 ("You must be born from above") and Matthew 28
("Go, therefore, and make disciples of all nations").

It is perhaps equally no surprise, then, that no topic at the
conference was livelier or more controversial than the priest's
relationship to Christ and its implications for his own identity
and ministry. Where the first day of the conference was
devoted to the cultural contexts and contemporary experiences
of priests, the second day took up the question, "As the church
moves forward, what does a good priest look like?" It explored
the priest as a "person" in relationship with Christ and himself,
as a "presbyter" in relationship with his bishop or superior and
his fellow priests, and as "pastor and priest" in relationship
with his parishioners and people. And, while "presbyteral"

concerns took up much of the day's time (and will be presented in the next chapter), discussion of "personal" ones touched perhaps the greatest depths of Christian and priestly life. We will examine issues of intimacy and sexuality in the fourth chapter, but first we turn to the two images that dominated the conference's discussion of the priest's relationship to Christ: disciple and icon. The two were in some tension, but, alongside their strengths and weaknesses, I hope to suggest a possible rapprochement.

Discipleship means "learning" or "following," and the priest, like any other Christian, is called to follow Christ. All are called to learn from him, to be challenged by him, to let themselves be formed by their ongoing encounter with him. A lifelong journey, discipleship aims at deep, lasting intimacy with Christ, whether that intimacy is construed as marriage or as friendship.

The priest's discipleship takes on a distinctive shape, however, because he is what several participants called a "public person" in the church and the world. By virtue of his ordination, he sacramentalizes communion with the bishop and the local church, as well as with the universal church. He leads the community and speaks and prays in its name. He represents the church in a public manner unlike the laity or even religious. He is not only a disciple, but also, again in a distinctive way, an apostle—not only called by Christ, but also sent by him to proclaim the gospel and build up the church. And, so, his discipleship has a uniquely public character. "I've watched them watch us . . . [looking for] leadership, discipleship, and service," as Mark Hession, pastor of Our Lady of Victory Parish in Centerville, Massachusetts, said about his parishioners in the aftermath of the sexual-abuse crisis.

"No one gives what one doesn't have," goes the Scholastic axiom, and thus the priest will founder if he is not a companion of Jesus. His public ministry will limp, as Rowan Williams described in this chapter's epigraph, to the degree that he is personally distant from the one who is the source of his life and ministry. Faithful discipleship is the sine qua non of the priesthood. To this end, several laypersons at the conference spoke of their desire for the priest to exemplify and teach the discipleship to which all believers are called. Carmen Mason, who has held numerous leadership positions in the San Antonio archdiocese, was asked by the conference organizers to sketch a portrait of the good priest. She mentioned the need for him to be a good preacher and evangelist, as well as having the ability to delegate and to relate well with different kinds of people, but, she said, "First and foremost, I think we would like to see a deep spirituality. Deep, abiding, intimate relation with God. Prayer on a daily basis, above and beyond the presiding of the sacraments that you might do on a daily basis. We would like to see men who go on retreats." Such visible prayerfulness, she said, is the fundamental condition for all of the priest's other activities.

A number of priests were equally insistent on the primacy of the priest's relationship with Christ. Donald Cozzens, the former rector of the diocesan seminary in Cleveland and the author of several books on priesthood and clerical culture, observed:

What is the chief characteristic that I'd be looking for in a candidate to the priesthood? Well, I'm going to steal the insight of Karl Rahner, who, to paraphrase him, said something like this, "The Christian of the twenty-first century will be a mystic or not at all." The word "mystic" is a little strong for me, so I'm going to soften that and say, "The Christian of the twenty-first century will be a contemplative or not at all." Do the candidates we have in formation for the priesthood, and do our priest-ministers today, do they have the depth of spiritual life that is evident when a person knows what contemplative prayer is? I think that kind of witness—a person who is leading an authentic life of the spirit, grounded in faith in Jesus Christ and really informed by the Spirit—is critical.

Dennis Sheehan noted that the priest inevitably suffers, however, from the same breakdown of faith that afflicts the entire church. "That's darkness," he said, and the church "has got to admit that the priests, as a group in the church—with some notable exceptions—may have to face up to the fact that they are affected by the same crisis of faith that's affecting our larger communities. And how we minister to, and how we move beyond, that is a real issue to me." In this context, the priest's discipleship, if not more demanding than that of the rest of the baptized, must be all the more visible and articulate:

> I would like to note here that I think one of the criteria for ordination—again, hard to authenticate—is that the individual presenting himself for ordination will have had a genuine personal—and I use the word "personal" not in the narrowly evangelical sense—experience of Jesus Christ. Now that's going to be varied. But it's a very legitimate question, and it's what some of the lay people sitting around the table

expressing their desire for the priest, in speaking of personal holiness, were talking about. Not just that the individual has really had an experience of conversion, but has the skill or the courage to share that with other people.

But, let's all realize that conversion is not [usually] like Paul getting knocked off the horse. Conversion is a daily struggle to conform to the image of Jesus Christ that the Holy Spirit is working within us to achieve. It's not something that's achieved overnight. So the conversion process will not produce a person of crystalline integrity. It will leave you with a person who has clay-feet, yet is struggling like all of us do, toward the realization of his Christian vocation in Jesus Christ. The difference, I think, is that with the priest people are looking to see that. And developing the skills of the priest to show that struggle of conversion in a real way is, I think, a challenge in priestly formation and a challenge for all of us. . . . The challenge remains that the people of God legitimately expect that the priest will be so focused on that journey [of conversion] that they will be able to see it in him.

Sheehan later expanded upon his comments at the conference in a keynote address given in 2004 to the National Catholic Educational Association.[2] Borrowing from the late Canadian Jesuit theologian Bernard Lonergan, he argued that conversion operates on several levels—the intellectual, moral, religious, and mystical—and that the seminary must do its part to foster a genuine transformation in each of them: "Is [the seminarian] just showing up and behaving suitably or is something deeper at work? Is he present for liturgy, prayer and retreats or is he engaged, moving, changing?" Building upon ten years of experience as the rector of two major seminaries, he argued that the present challenge is that, whereas in the past seminarians were much younger and came to seminary with lengthy immersion in "Catholic stuff," today's seminarians are older and often lack a systematic exposure to that "stuff." Thus, while in years past seminary formation could effect a comprehensive transformation in which the seminarian's human and spiritual formation tracked each other—one's identity was really and radically shaped in the seminary—contemporary formation more often works with an already largely formed personality, one much more experienced, for good and for bad, and one in which it can be "far more difficult to change basic assumptions." In particular, Sheehan said, some of these older seminarians may find it harder to let seminary formation expand their understanding of the priesthood; they may satisfactorily perform required tasks, yet fail to be sufficiently transformed in mind and heart. The result is that the seminary will often produce a "formed priest who is only a partial Christian." Not in the sense that the newly ordained priest's personal devotion to Christ is necessarily inauthentic or absent, for it can often be intense and even dramatic, but that it will lack deep roots and insufficiently shape the entirety of the priest's life. Such lack of comprehensive, ongoing conversion reveals itself, he argued, in needlessly divisive leadership and unimaginative, wandering preaching.

Sheehan acknowledged the difficulty of measuring conversion in seminary formation—above all in respect for the difference between the internal and external forums—but advised changing canon law where necessary to permit some sort of public insight into the seminarian's journey of conversion. A possible model, he suggested, might be the annual or regular "manifestation of conscience" to one's superior practiced in many religious communities. Whatever instruments of discernment are developed, the goal of seminary formation and, *a fortiori*, the priest's life, must be conversion to discipleship:

> Holy and healthy. Both are grounded in the inner life of mind, spirit, and soul. The keys to holiness and inner, total health lie below the readily observable surface of life and behavior. It is a challenge to the church and to its schools of priestly preparation to be able not only to measure skills and behaviors but to say to the church on the day of ordination: here is a disciple, here is a soul formed in the image of Christ. I am suggesting more attention to conversion as a way to move in this direction.

The comments by Mason, Cozzens, and Sheehan found broad acceptance—who, after all, is against the priest being conformed more closely to Christ?—but some participants pointed out the potential limits of the discipleship model. For one, the priest is both disciple and apostle. Discipleship is his most basic identity as a Christian, but he is also called and empowered through ordination to act in the name of Christ and the apostles. Along these lines, William Morell, O.M.I., then-rector of the Oblate School of Theology and now American vicar provincial of his religious order, added that the popular model of the priest as a servant-leader has often tilted heavily to servant, thereby obscuring the priest's sacramental charge of public, communal leadership—a loss that has had detrimental effects on both the church and the priesthood. An emphasis on equality in discipleship can likewise lead to an effacement or even abdication of priestly difference, which in turn can lead to an embarrassed, apologetic sense of priestly identity. Susan Wood, whose preparatory paper took pains to stress the enduring baptismal relationship between the priest and the laity, nonetheless cautioned about the dangers of conflating discipleship and ministry, and of misusing the word "ministry" either too restrictively (as with the Vatican's 1997 "Instruction on Certain Questions Regarding the Collaboration of the Non-Ordained Faithful in the Sacred Ministry of Priests") or too expansively (viewing lectors or ushers as ministers):

> I do think priests are disciples, but they are disciples out of their baptismal character, as my paper represented. And I think ministry differs from discipleship in that it's an add-on to discipleship. . . . I wouldn't want to just reduce a priest to being a very nice disciple, who is humble and keeps his head down and does his work. Because in some sense [he's] the church coming to visibility. . . . And [priests] are not public just because they stand in a pulpit and preach on Sunday and have a large congregation listening to them. They are public persons because they're representative of the church and in a sense sacramentalize the community in its communion with other communities.

There is a need, then, for the discipleship model to be complemented by a clear sense of priestly identity and even distinctiveness. These two aims are not irreconcilable. Donald Wolf, for instance, noted the irony that the Southern Baptist Church in his town, Duncan, Oklahoma, has produced over the last twenty years more priests and nuns than the two diocesan high schools, which have a yearly enrollment of over a thousand students. This disparity, he claimed, is due to the Baptists' focus on conversion and the demanding, public character of Christian discipleship, which then can lead to a greater appreciation of the particular demands of priestly and religious life.

The question of priestly discipleship points to a deeper one of priestly identity. Although it is true that the ordained priesthood is essentially ministerial—and the priest sanctified primarily through the exercise of that ministry, as Vatican II held (*Presbyterorum ordinis*, 12–13)—priestly identity can't be limited to one's activity. Cletus Kiley put it thusly:

> A priest is and a priest does. And I think the "is" part is something we need to keep looking at. Monsignor Cummings was eighty-two years old, a retired founding pastor, living in the rectory, and an invalid. He didn't say Mass, he didn't preach, he didn't do a damn thing anymore. Was he a good priest and a good pastoral presence? Stunningly so. And no one could say he wasn't a good priest. But he didn't do anything anymore, he didn't really have a ministry, at least not a public one. . . . The identity is something deeper, and it's rooted in this identification with Christ.

Gerald Fogarty sounded a similar note in describing the difference he sees between the Catholic and Protestant ordained ministers who are faculty members in the University of Virginia's religious studies department. As a Catholic priest, he stated, "I realize the radical difference in their [Protestant] approach and mine. There is the notion of permanency—to use the old term, the character [imprinted through holy orders]. I am in a permanent relationship within the church as an institution and as mystical body."

This discussion of priestly identity was catalyzed by Paul Griffiths's proposal that the priest be seen as an "icon of Christ." Taking up the conference's guiding question—"What does the good priest look like?"— he said, with customary provocation and acuity:

> I think that most fundamentally the priest does look like an icon. An icon is a visible object, an object that is characterized by being ordered, beautiful, but most importantly an object that displaces the gaze from itself to that of which it is an icon. So if the priest is iconic for the people, the priest is iconic of Jesus Christ. And that means that in his very mode of being and in his actions, he displaces the gaze of the people from himself to Christ.
>
> Now, it seems to me . . . that the moment at which the iconic function, the iconic being—both being and function we need here—of the priest is most evident when the priest celebrates the Eucharistic liturgy. In that event the priest is iconic in the strict and full sense. Speaking for myself, but I think not just for myself, what people most desperately need from our priests is that they do in fact function iconically for us. That seems to me essential. It is fundamental to every-

thing else the priests are and do when they function iconically for their people. They form and conform the people to what they, in fact, are, which is the body of Christ. So that the iconic presence of the priest in the congregation is a principle, not only a simple instrument, by which that congregation is conformed to Christ's body.

Now there is another characteristic of icons, and that is that they don't actually do very much. They just are. There they are.... [E]specially given the changes in numbers of priestly vocations and so on and so forth, it seems abundantly obvious to me that to be a true icon of Christ to the people, priests need to do vastly less than they do. And the only way that can happen is if their iconic function to the people forms and conforms people, the laity, to do vastly more than we do [presently]. So again, what would happen if a priest were really an icon, is [that] the priests would simply be. You don't actually have to do anything. And three cheers if that could happen.

These comments provoked the most heated exchanges by far of the conference. Ernesto Cortés warned, for instance, that some priests might use such theology to become lazy or self-indulgent:

One of the difficulties I have about this notion of icons is that unfortunately for some of the younger priests I have to deal with, if we start talking about them being icons, they are going to become self-righteous, self-absorbed, pietistic.... I mean, there's a big cultural gap between the priests who are now being ordained—at least in my experiences—a lot of very suburban, a lot of very privileged backgrounds, and the guys who used to work seventy to eighty hours a week, you had to get them to take a day off, and had to remind them that, "You know, Father, you can't just work yourself to death." And there's a big cultural divide, so be real careful, it seems to me, when you start using that kind of [iconic] language.

The most pronounced concerns about iconicity were that (1) it would place priests on a pedestal above their people, leading to a renewed clericalism, and (2) it might foster a quietist withdrawal by the priest and the church, removing them from engagement with the broader world. On the first point, we should recall from the previous chapter the comments by Susan Wood and other participants on the iconicity of every Christian, who through baptism is truly and fully an *alter Christus*. Vatican II, Wood wrote, generally avoided calling priests "other Christs," preferring instead the more careful language of the priest as one who acts *in persona Christi capitis*—in the person of Christ, the head of the church.

Still others wondered how one could even translate iconicity into a practical and practicable life as a diocesan priest in a parish. Sidney Callahan, a psychologist and writer, suggested instead viewing the priest as a friend who bears a family resemblance to Jesus. Borrowing from Julian of Norwich, she said that the priest should reveal God's "courtesy" in his respectful, listening openness to others. Moreover, where evil is always "very conforming, very narrowing," genuine happiness—which follows from being closely related to Jesus—

brings immense variety; upending Tolstoy's famous dictum in *Anna Karenina*, Callahan said that "all happy families are different," and that the priest must see himself as one who helps to foster equality and diversity within the church family. On a related note, John Strynkowski observed, in comments that will be taken up in greater detail in chapter 4, that the people also form the priest; drawing on his forty years as a diocesan priest, he insisted that their iconic, formative relationship is much more of a two-way street than Griffiths indicated in his remarks. Iconicity, these and other participants cautioned, can easily lead to a clericalist, paternalist conception of the priesthood and the church.

Such triumphalism might also feed a second temptation of the iconic model: a quietist withdrawal into an ecclesial womb separated from involvement with the world. The tension at the conference over the priest as icon, while perhaps prone to abstraction and pastoral irrelevance, revealed just how powerfully images of Christ, church, and mission shape one another. It disclosed, I think, deeper, perennial tensions over the nature of the church and its ministry: the relationships between church and world, liturgy and justice, being and doing, action and contemplation, communion and mission, cultic and servant-leader models of priesthood.

Philip Murnion and Paul Griffiths, in an intense, respectful exchange, stood as exemplars of these tensions:

Paul Griffiths: There is something the priest is supposed to do. And I still think that it is to image Christ as icon to the congregation. It is not to transform the world in accord with some political vision. It is not to comment learnedly or not on controversial matters of the day. Those are things that the Body of Christ, the laity, are called to do. So one thing I would like is that priests would figure out what the job is that they have to do and do that one, not some other one.

Philip Murnion: The concern I have, Paul, is what imaging Christ means. It sounds very placid, it sounds very, in your terms, iconic. But what Christ does he image? And it seems to me that a priest who's about empowering the people that transform the social structures is part of the Christ he wants to image. One that says this world is to be redeemed, this world is to be transformed, human dignity is to be central to everything that we do. Maybe you were saying that, but I find that the people find the priest resembling Christ when he works as hard as they do, [when he tries to] figure out how to balance the various parts of his life and yet do so in such a way that it brings them forward to take responsibility. I'm not arguing that he should be at every meeting or the like, or run the community or organizations or the like, but he should be a man of the world—he is secular, not remote. He shares the struggles of the local community and of the larger political and social community. So, I don't know—maybe I'm not catching what you're saying and maybe I'm arguing against something you're not trying to say.

Griffiths: Well, maybe I'm not sure either. I suppose it's a fundamental theological judgment, right? I mean, it seems to me that the central ministry of the priest, at least the congregational parish priest, is to the congregation and not to the world. Whereas, by contrast, the mission of the baptized is to the world. And, so, it is as simple as that.

Murnion: Except that the way in which the congregation gets into the world is sometimes if the priest creates a situation where they are encouraged to get some basis in Catholic social teaching, get some skills to get operative in the world. So, yes, it is [the laity's] role in the world, but who is going to move their role in the world if [the priest's] not seeing them as apostolic, as going forward, and helping them to go forward?

The differing emphases between the two men were clear. To use the categories mentioned above, Murnion spoke more in terms of world, justice, doing, action, mission, and service; Griffiths, in terms of church, liturgy, being, contemplation, communion, and worship. Murnion viewed the priest as an activist engaged in the work of justice, empowering his people to transform the world and advance human dignity; not content to stay in the rectory or the chapel, his priest goes out into the streets and fields to organize and rally. Griffiths, by contrast, saw the priest as a contemplative, drawing his people into communion with Christ through worship and then sending them into the world. He, like the sister Mary in Luke's Gospel, is to remind the Marthas in the church and the world of the "one thing necessary," which is sitting at the feet of Jesus and gazing at him, being receptive to his very presence.

Underlying these polarities or tensions is the foundational

question on which Murnion put his finger: "But what Christ does he image?" In other words, the priest's vision of Jesus shapes the whole of his life and ministry. Murnion inclined more to a "synoptic" Jesus, who teaches, heals, exorcizes; Griffiths to a "Johannine" Jesus, dramatic in his self-possession and meditativeness. Faced with such marked contrasts, we can only be grateful that the early church rejected Tatian's *Diatessaron* and its attempt to synthesize the four Gospels into one handy product!

My own sense, unsurprisingly, is that these tensions can be fruitful if they are first cleared of misconceptions and exaggerations. In this regard, the extemporaneous nature of the conference and its large size necessarily hindered the precision and comprehensiveness one would legitimately expect in a more academic setting. Griffiths, for instance, offered too neat a distinction between church and world, one rooted perhaps in his Johannine vision of Christ. Although Vatican II taught that the laity have a particular calling to transform the world—they are uniquely "secular" in comparison to the other members of the church (*Lumen gentium*, 31; *Apostolicam actuositatem*, 2)—it also held that the church as a whole has a worldly mission (*Gaudium et spes*, 40). The equation clergy–church : laity–world is incomplete and inadequate. Thus, the priest, precisely as an icon of Christ, is called to act in "worldly" ways; his iconicity extends beyond the liturgical into literally mundane matters, even if its deepest roots are sacramental. Murnion, for his part, advanced a somewhat one-sided view of the church's engagement with the world, identifying it too strongly with a kind of social and political activism. I think here of Vatican II's statement that the Eucharist is the "source and summit" of the church's life.

Murnion's comments could give the impression that worship is a fueling-up or a preparation for the "real world" outside of the liturgy. The church, however, is never more real or more fully itself than when it celebrates the Eucharist; while the church is made for mission, that mission has its foundation and fulfillment in the communion made possible by Christ alone. Murnion readily acknowledged this point elsewhere in the conference, when he said of the priest's ministry that "the heart of it—as Bob [Imbelli] was reminding us—is the relationship of that priest to Jesus: Jesus personally, Jesus in sacrament, Jesus in community, Jesus in this world."

In light of the comments of Griffiths and Murnion, then, I would argue that while the image of the priest as icon of Christ has its limits and its dangers, it nonetheless does not necessarily place the priest on a pedestal or remove him or the church from its mission in the world. It must, however, like any model, including that of discipleship, remain open to the full sweep of the Gospel accounts of Jesus. And that Christic tension must not be relaxed, however tempting or understandable it might be, if the priest's life and ministry are to be fruitful for the church and the world.

If these tensions remain perennial, I think that a rapprochement between discipleship and iconicity can be found in the reality of suffering and failure in the priest's life. There is no authentic Christian existence that does not pass through the heart of the paschal mystery. "The Cross," as Yves Congar wrote in recalling the suffering he endured on account of his theological labors, "is a condition of every holy work."[3] Failure was necessarily a prominent topic at a conference held in the immediate aftermath of the clerical sexual-abuse crisis, but a number of participants went beyond boilerplate or clichéd statements into true wisdom. The most perceptive insight, I think, came from John Strynkowski, who was charged with responding to Enda McDonagh's paper, "The Risk of Priesthood." He began by observing that much talk of the "good priest" and his characteristics is often misleading, even dangerous: "When we give people the illusion that by acquiring a certain set of skills [in the seminary] they will therefore be successful, we're failing them." After noting various kinds of failure—professional, pastoral, moral—he pushed to its deepest level:

> But there's also a further reason for a recognition of failure, and that is in terms of spirituality. After all, we live because of a catastrophic failure. We live because of the Cross. The Cross was a failure. It was folly and failure. Christ was seen as a failure on the Cross. And yet, out of that failure came life; out of that failure came victory. And so the good priest, it seems to me, is someone who has drunk deeply of the paschal mystery, and recognizes that God's ways are not human ways. They are not the ways of success. God raises up the lowly; God raises up those who in the history of salvation were deemed the humble, the poor, the marginalized. God raises up Christ from the dead. From what had been perceived as a failure, there is where triumph is.

Karl Rahner, in an essay on the priesthood, wrote (and I paraphrase), "The priest of the future will earn his keep to the extent to which the Gospel has passed through his heart." And so he is someone who has absorbed in his own experience, in his own prayer, in his own life, the radicalness of the paschal mystery—failure and triumph. There's also, in some discussion of priesthood, the use of ontological terminology. But one of the other things we have to also remember is that in contingent being itself, there is inevitable failure. To be contingent means to fail. We are all going to fail in health; and we're all going to die. . . . There's going to be conflict. We can only do so much. There is also the immense *mysterium iniquitatis*, the mystery of evil. The mystery of evil still holds its sway. Not simply in society, not simply in culture, but also in the church. And we inevitably are going to fail in terms of that. There are going to be moments in our lives when we are rendered helpless by the mystery of evil, when we do not succeed. We fail in the face of the mystery of evil, no matter how much we struggle against it.

And so recognition of failure is something that, it seems to me, is more than a [mere] component of the life of the good priest as the church moves forward. But that again is what everyone experiences. And insofar as the priest recognizes the possibility and reality of failure, then he has entered into greater solidarity with the rest of the human race, and becomes more compassionate, becomes a better servant by that recognition of failure. In the back of my mind as I read Enda's paper, what came to my mind and provoked [these comments] was *The Diary of a Country Priest* by [Georges] Bernanos, who, dying, recognizes himself a failure and, yet, here's the great irony and the great wonder, he is able to say, "Grace is everywhere."

In their emphasis on the paradox of the paschal mystery—at once "failure and triumph"—Strynkowski's comments strike me as a gloss on Hebrews' meditations on the priest's humanity and its saving role:

> For it is clear that [Christ] did not come to help angels, but the descendants of Abraham. Therefore he had to become like his brothers and sisters in every respect, so that he might be a merciful and faithful high priest in the service of God, to make a sacrifice of atonement for the sins of the people. Because he himself was tested by what he suffered, he is able to help those who are being tested. (Hebrews 2:16–18)

Although this passage refers to Christ, it applies no less to the Catholic priest as a standard of his life and ministry. The priest, in a special way, must know his weakness and vulnerability before Christ (and the church). Iconicity must not place the priest on a pedestal but plunge him more deeply into Christ's paschal mystery and his people's share in it. The genuine priestly icon of Christ, then, is one who in Christ has shared fully the joys and sufferings of humanity. "Tested in every way," he can "deal gently with the ignorant and the wayward, since he himself is subject to weakness" (Hebrews 4:15; 5:2). Transparent and humble, he will avoid triumphalism and that peculiar, even perverse self-inflation that masks itself with the rhetoric of service and littleness (as when, for example, a bishop speaks of the "privilege of being your servant"). Versed in weakness, he knows God's ever-greater grace.

In this context, the priest's acceptance of his failure and weakness is decidedly neither an invitation to mediocrity nor an acquiescence to sin. In the midst of the sexual-abuse scandals and widespread dissatisfaction with priestly performance, higher standards of professionalism and accountability are clearly needed. Peter Steinfels's *A People Adrift* has powerful words about the virtually complete lack of accountability—professional and personal—in priestly life; ordination effectively confers a "lifetime license" with few corresponding standards of service. Nor should the acknowledgment of failure involve a trivializing or rationalization of sin. In *View from the Altar: Reflections on the Rapidly Changing Catholic Priesthood*, Howard Bleichner, a seminary rector for twenty years, argues that the influence in postconciliar seminaries of the humanistic psychology of Carl Rogers and the self-actualization theory of Abraham Maslow contributed to a weakening of moral standards. Notwithstanding the merits of these theories, objective norms of sinfulness gave way to a developmental continuum, in which "'sins' [were] regarded as setbacks on the road to ever greater progress." Such theories had "little time for mortal sin, and no time at all for original sin," and could not but help contribute to a climate of moral laxity—and, later, scandal—in seminaries and the priesthood.[4]

Faced with such mediocrity and scandal, the priest's call to holiness takes on even greater weight. He is to be an icon of discipleship, the one who leads the community—as he must, because his ordination empowers him to act "in the person of Christ the Head"—by the witness of his life. Although his authority comes from God through ordination, it becomes effective to the extent that it is earned, rather than assumed. Mindful of his ordained status, he must not forget the more fundamental equality and identity of being he shares with other Christians through baptism. The priest, like any other

Christian, most resembles Christ by virtue of his baptism; his ordination is a further specification of that resemblance, not its replacement or overwriting. Peter Casarella, a theologian at the Catholic University of America, offered a beautiful image of the paradox of the priest as icon and disciple, as unique and united:

> The priest stands in the Eucharist in the person of Christ the head, which means then that the priest in a unique fashion, in a fashion different from the participation of the laity, reenacts Christ's *eucharistia*— Christ's thanksgiving to the Father. He alone performs the words of Institution. . . . [And, yet,] even as the priest appears to the assembly in a unique role, he is also kneeling in his heart. He is also in some sense silently, secretly, hiddenly, one with the laity. There is a silent, wordless prayer of the baptized Christian in the priest celebrating the Mass.

Thus, even at the climax of the church's life, the priest lives in Christ at the intersection of glory and weakness. Casarella said elsewhere at the conference that the mark of a true icon is the self-effacement of both the artist and the image: "It's really in the shabbiness of the priest that God appears. It's really in the mundaneness, the everyday encounter, and the fact that he's there with his people, that God literally speaks in the icon." Dennis Sheehan, while expressing some hesitation over the rhetoric of priestly iconicity—he got a laugh when he recalled his mother's words: "If you think I'm going to burn a candle in front of your picture, you're crazy"—nonetheless agreed that iconicity is a lifelong project of being conformed to the image of Christ, which takes form not in paint and wood but in flesh and blood. And, to the extent that a priest is iconic or sacramental in that discipleship, people can see in his struggles and successes a window into Christ himself. His life and experiences—certainly of victory but even of failure—then become not a barrier but a bridge to Christ. This mediating presence, as Rowan Williams noted, is none other than the very heart of the priesthood of Jesus Christ.

Chapter Three

The Priest as Presbyter

One priest said to me when he was celebrating his 25th anniversary, [that] he wasn't sure he would have done it again if he had known how things would turn out to be. I said, "What do you mean?" And he said, "Well, I thought we were in this together. I thought there was a corporate mission that we are all contributing to. [But] I'm left entirely to my own to decide what my mission is, what my parish is, what my spirituality is, what my anything is." And he does it very well, but that's not what he signed on for. He signed on for some corporate mission.

—Philip Murnion

"Only connect." E. M. Forster used these words as the epigraph to *Howards End*, his novel on the difficulties—and possibilities—of bridging the social, cultural, and simple human divides that separate us from one another. The desire to connect stands at the heart of every person. Psychiatrists and psychologists, for instance, see isolation and social withdrawal as classic symptoms of clinical depression. Aristotle's *Politics* held that a self-sufficient being was not human but a beast or a god, and Christianity has gone still further in affirming that God's own reality is wholly social. Communion, the particularly Christian way of speaking of such divine and human relationality, lies at the heart of personal and priestly identity, and the priest is one whose calling is to foster that communion within the church and in the world. The priest, a "man of communion," is to be a "servant of communion."

That identity and service, however, are fraught with difficulties. Some problems, such as ecclesial conflict and the reality of failure in the priest's life, are perennial. Other tensions, such as the "adulthood" of the laity and increasing diversity in the church, are more contextual. Priests of all ages today find themselves facing immense changes in church and society: older priests, ordained for service in one church (the preconciliar) with one set of expectations, find themselves ministering in another (the postconciliar) with often quite different ones; some middle-aged priests are demoralized over a perceived betrayal of Vatican II by a succession of popes and their episcopal appointees; and younger priests strive to minister in a culture that is often deeply skeptical of their commitments and in a presbyterate that can regard many of them with suspicion and even acrimony.

The conference addressed many of these tensions head-on. While the comments—as did the participants—tilted to the middle-aged and liberal, the overriding tenor was nonideological; the participants on the whole were more concerned with addressing relational problems than with pushing particular agendas. The emphasis fell therefore not on the prospects of married and female priests or on the need for "orthodox" bishops and priests, for example, but on issues of communication and character. If this led to a lack of polemical fireworks, I would argue that the gains in insight were preferable.

This chapter, then, looks at the priest in his relationships with his bishop or religious superior and with his fellow priests. Summarizing and commenting on some of the main themes that arose at the conference, it explores the priest as a "man of communion."

Bishops

Most Catholic laity have virtually no interaction with their bishop apart from the sacrament of confirmation and the occasional fundraiser. In many large dioceses, however, even the priests may often have little personal contact with him, meeting instead with auxiliary bishops and chancery staff. This distance has its good and bad aspects. Several New York priests, for instance, have said that they liked the late Cardinal John O'Connor because he left them alone and didn't micromanage their parishes and initiatives; he also had a weekly open-door policy for all of his priests. Gerald Fogarty, a Jesuit historian of American Catholicism who teaches at the University of Virginia, told a story at the conference that, while exaggerated and perhaps even true, lends some humorous perspective:

Some time around 1947, Cardinal Spellman was visiting parishes on the other side of the Hudson [River], but still within the archdiocese. And he found out there was a church in this one town. And he said, "I didn't know we had a parish there." And so he stopped off, and this man came out dressed in old khaki trousers and a sweatshirt, and Cardinal Spellman said,

"I'm Cardinal Spellman, the archbishop of New York." And the priest said, "Whatever happened to Hayes [Spellman's predecessor as cardinal archbishop]?"

That benign anonymity, however apocryphal it may be, is history. The conference could scarcely have taken place at a lower point in the history of bishop–priest relationships in the American church. The sexual-abuse crisis wounded the entire church, of course, but priests were particularly hurt. They suffered not only the humiliation of guilt-by-association with their abusive brothers, but also the anger prompted by the belief—shared by many observers—that the 2002 Charter for the Protection of Children and Young People was partly an effort by the bishops to save their own hides in the court of public opinion by sacrificing their priests. The Charter, it seemed, compromised priests' rights to due process and a good reputation in face of allegations of abuse, and placed the bishop in an adversarial role with his priests; their relationship shifted from the sacramental and social realms to the legal and corporate. Despite subsequent revisions of the Charter and the passage of time, these tensions remain palpable to the present day.

The uneasy relationship between priests and bishops has historical roots, extending well beyond the immediate problems of the sexual-abuse crisis. Gerald Fogarty sketched this history in his preparatory paper, "Priests and Their Bishops and People in the American Church." Ranging from the establishment of Catholicism in Maryland to the postconciliar period, he observed that priests went "from being the most educated men in a predominantly ethnic community in the city . . . [to serving] ethnically mixed parishes in the suburbs." Throughout, the relationship between priests and bishops has been marked by recurrent tensions over priests' role in the selection of bishops and their rights vis-à-vis their bishops. John Carroll, the first American bishop, was elected with Roman permission by his fellow priests in 1789, and Rome simply confirmed that election. His election, though, was unique, and, during the nineteenth century, priests' rights of episcopal nomination were variously suppressed and supported. By 1916, however, these rights were revoked by Rome, partly in response to the Americanist crisis and to instances of politicking (as in the selection in 1915 of Brooklyn auxiliary George Mundelein as archbishop of Chicago). I would add that this was not the last time that Chicago political machinations would have national, even international, implications!

Alongside the selection of bishops, Fogarty noted the difficulties in establishing a system of clerical discipline in a country that was considered mission territory until 1908. Despite the demise of lay trusteeism, wherein the laity of a given parish were responsible for administering its temporal affairs (often including the hiring and dismissal of clergy), Bishop John England, of Charleston, South Carolina, supported a modified republican governance that allowed for substantial priestly and lay participation in diocesan life; he retained full authority over his diocese but actively sought structured consultation in his ministry. Such initiatives soon died out, and tensions arose over priests' tenure in, and removal from, office. Priest–bishop conflict reached such a point that Rome installed an apostolic delegate (later *nuncio*) in 1893, partly in order to resolve such disputes.

The history outlined by Fogarty stretches both back to

the early church—as even the most cursory reading of Paul's letters reveals—and forward to the present day. We will examine these contemporary tensions between priests and bishops from both sides, beginning with the bishops.

A bishop's most important ecclesial relationship is to his priests, who, theologically and pastorally, are his presence in the parishes of his diocese. If a bishop loses that relationship, his ministry can be fatally compromised. Sharon Euart, R.S.M., a canon lawyer and former associate general secretary of the USCCB, noted the primacy of the bishop's relationship with his priests and of the bishops' overwhelming desire to make that relationship work:

> One of my experiences I've really loved was being part of these workshops that Notre Dame put on for new bishops. And it was just a wonderful opportunity for bishops to come together, all of whom were new, some as ordinaries, and others as auxiliaries, but terribly open to finding out how to do it. And for many of them, and I would say for most of them, the most important concern was, how do I make it with my priests? What can I do to get to know them better, to understand them better, and to enhance the relationship they have? So I want to offer that as an opportunity to say that I think that there's a genuine interest in wanting to do what's best on the part of the bishops.

Both bishop and priest participants at the conference indicated the often severe stresses, perennial or situational, on that relationship. Dennis Sheehan, for instance, noted the difficulties inherent in the bishop being at the same time a leader and a friend to his priests:

> The bishop is in a very difficult, ambiguous situation with regard to his priests on a human level. If he gets too human with them, maybe it gets in the way of his being a leader in the presbyterate. I don't honestly think that that's a necessary tension. I know bishops who have overcome it, who have a very healthy, good, mature relationship with the majority of their priests, and yet who are able to lead their priests very much when that's called for. But on the other hand, bishops, like priests, are limited human beings, and not all of them have the skill to manage that very tricky kind of impasse: how to establish a human relationship with your priests and still maintain your stature as leader.

Donald Cozzens said that the "impasse" mentioned by Sheehan was complicated by the social tensions inherent in an unequal relationship. Priests often speak of loneliness and isolation, he said, but it is bishops who are "perhaps the loneliest people in the world, at least in the ecclesial world":

> I think it's very tricky for priests to relate with their bishops on a level of friendship. First of all, if a priest tends to include his bishop in various social activities, he's afraid it might be perceived as climbing. And to refer to miter envy and miter ambition, I think there's a fair amount of that.
>
> Human sexuality is very much at the heart of being a human. At the same time there is another drive that

doesn't get much attention and that's the drive of ambition. I once asked a young man, "You know, I think you have all the characteristics necessary to be a priest. Have you ever thought of the priesthood?" He said, "No, no, Father, I haven't thought of the priesthood." He said, "I want to be a bishop." Well, a lot of priests do not want to be bishops. But I think a lot of us want to be asked. So we can [then] say, "No, no." So that whole idea of going somewhere is an issue. And I think it's tricky on the part of bishops to invite a priest or a few priests out to dinner and the theater or the orchestra or a movie for fear that they are going to say yes because the bishop asked them. So the whole relationship of bishop to priest, I think, is very, very tricky.

Cozzens also spoke of the priest's relationship to his bishop and to his brother priests (which we will take up later in this chapter), but it should be noted here that his remarks on ambition and envy struck an extraordinarily deep chord among the priests at the conference and prompted numerous replies. It was abundantly clear that he had identified something essential in the experiences of bishops and priests.

Alongside Sheehan's and Cozzens's comments, Jeremiah Boland, the director of priest personnel in the Chicago archdiocese, spoke of the vulnerability inherent in the episcopal office itself, as well as in the holder of that office. He offered the example of Cardinal Bernardin:

As I was reflecting this past week on the topic of, "What does a good priest look like?" in terms of his relationship with the bishop and with brother priests,

I couldn't help but think of the one whose legacy and spirit and vision brings many of us around this table. Not just Jesus, but Cardinal Bernardin. And so much of his life was devoted to the relationship of a bishop to his priests and he was so concerned about the spirit of a presbyterate. If you're like me, there have been many times in the past several months, when I've wondered what it would be like if Joseph was still with us. Would we be at a different place trying to sort through this horrific chapter? I would like to think and believe in my heart that we would be, and we miss his voice terribly.

In the aftermath of the [sexual-abuse] allegation and his own illness, the cardinal was many things to us Chicago priests. But many would say it was in the midst of the allegation and the illness that he became a pastor; that the sheer circumstances of these events invited him to be vulnerable in a way that deconstructed some of the defenses and some of the things that perhaps kept him distant in terms of how he related to priests, bishops, and to anyone. And this sense of vulnerability became an occasion that so tremendously enhanced his influence on priests, the city of Chicago, and, in fact, the world. And I think there is something to be learned about that as we deal with some of the tensions in the church right now.

To say that the relationship between priests and bishops is under duress would be an understatement. In fact, there are dioceses in this country where the relationship is so fractured, I'm not sure where to go. This last autumn [2002] I was at the meeting of the

National Association of Church Personnel and Administrators and there was a track for priests involved in personnel work. And it was just breathtaking, the lack of confidence that some of the priests felt about their bishop's ability to deal with this crisis. It was in some ways frightening, this feeling of, "We're not sure of where we are going to go." In the past couple weeks I've had the opportunity to speak with three different ordinaries, and I can't even imagine what their world is like. One bishop, who has been rather stoic through all this, said, "It's just finally gotten to me. I can't sleep at night, I feel like I'm walking on eggshells, I don't know when the next shoe is going to drop." Another bishop, who has been pilloried in the press, and by most accounts in a very unfair way, seemed to me to be almost about to dissolve in tears just not knowing what to do. And I thought to myself later, gosh, if he could share this with his priests he would be surrounded by a support that he has never known in his ministry.

These comments on vulnerability call to mind Cardinal Bernardin's account in *The Gift of Peace* of the transformation wrought by the challenge he received from some younger priests while he was still archbishop of Cincinnati. He had noticed that in the course of his ministry and good works he was not setting aside sufficient time for personal prayer, and so he felt hypocritical in urging others to pray. At dinner one evening, he told the priests of his difficulties with prayer and asked for their help. They asked him if he was serious and, once assured of his desire, "blunt[ly]" told him that he could not tell others about the priority of prayer, if he was not himself spending significant "quality time" with the Lord. Thus challenged, he soon resolved to spend the first hour of every day in prayer, a discipline he practiced to the end of his life. That vulnerability, that willingness to subject himself to criticism and even embarrassment transformed his life and ministry, bearing its ultimate fruit in his saintly response to terminal cancer and a false allegation of sexual abuse. One can only imagine what a risk it must have been for a young archbishop known for his administrative competence and even ambition to acknowledge his lack of prayerfulness and to place himself at the mercy of his priests, especially younger ones. The cardinal was saved by his vulnerability to his priests.

Boland's comments also revealed how perennial problems in the priest–bishop relationship—inequality, ambition, envy, favoritism, vulnerability—are compounded by more situational ones. To this end, several participants spoke of the isolation generated by the bishop being an outsider in his diocese and by the size—either geographically or demographically—of a given diocese. Think, for instance, of the different difficulties and possibilities facing Chicago with its 944 diocesan priests and 373 parishes, and Shreveport with its 42 diocesan priests and 32 parishes. Or, geographically, of the differences between Bridgeport in Connecticut (633 square miles) and Cheyenne in Wyoming (97,548 square miles). Every diocese has its own challenges, but these can be complicated when the bishop finds himself distanced from his priests and people through sheer numbers or miles. When that isolation is compounded by overwork, the bishop's life can become overwhelming. Addressing these concerns, Archbishop Oscar Lipscomb of Mobile said:

Well, I'm not the one to speak of loneliness from a bishop's perspective. I'm in my own hometown. I knew all of the presbyterate at one time better than I do now, but I've ordained the ones that have come along since I've been there, so I know them, too. But there is a kind of loneliness that I have personally not experienced, but have found in some of my brothers by way of contrast, and you're quite right. We do need to make some kind of an opening to each other. How it happens depends upon the circumstance. I've already given my opinion that from where I'm sitting, Mobile is just about the right size. We have half the state of Alabama, and about 70,000 Catholics, about 85,000 if you count the marvelous Hispanic influx that has happened these past two years, that we still haven't come to terms with, but we're trying.

But in the midst of that kind of small church, you do have a sense of who everybody is, and you're able to sum that up. I would frankly be at a loss without that kind of personal [knowledge]. I don't need a file when I need to talk about a priest. I know everything that there is, and I don't think that most people like that, but that's [the way it is]. . . . [Y]ou see them all twice a year, once a year. But you're a hometown boy, too. And that makes another difference. No one had to instruct us, [unlike] bishops coming in to a diocese where they've never been before and have no idea.

Archbishop Lipscomb added that a bishop coming from outside the diocese could and does often greatly succeed, but the point remains: a bishop should generally come from his own diocese—and stay in his diocese. Familiarity, intimacy, and commitment are essential to any relationship, especially the bishop's to his diocese, which Christian tradition has long likened to Christ's marriage to his church.

Priests, for their part, mentioned at the conference a number of problems, the first of which was lack of trust in their bishops and their ability to address the sexual-abuse crisis. The Boston archdiocese remains unique in the ferocity of the damage inflicted by the crisis and its aftermath, but the following comment by Francis Kelley, a priest of that archdiocese, found acceptance among many participants:

> When I was doing stuff with programs with clergy, I had a question asked: with whom do you identify as a priest—with the bishop or with the people? And, some priests would want to answer: both. And I said, "Well, you can't say both, answer the question." And when it came down to it they said, "Oh yeah, with the people, definitely. My identity as a priest is tied up with the people." After everything broke in Boston, there's no hesitation when that question gets put up. So there's a breaking of trust in terms of the identity of the priest with the bishop. I don't know how it is in the rest of the country, but with us it just doesn't exist anymore.

If Kelley's way of posing the question is theologically inadequate, since the priest is inseparably related to both his bishop and his people, it nonetheless reflects the pastoral reality faced by many priests. Several priest-participants expressed a lack of confidence in the bishops' ability to deal with the sexual-abuse crisis, while others felt that some of the bishops were more interested in pleasing Rome than in honestly addressing pastoral problems such as the declining number of priests and seminarians (a concern which, it should be noted, cannot be reduced to advocacy for married priests, but must instead take into account—as Andrew Greeley argues—the reluctance of most priests to actively promote priestly vocations[1]).

The sense that a number of bishops are more concerned with the Vatican than with their priests and dioceses was expressed by Philip Murnion, who spoke of the recent history of episcopal appointments in the United States:

> We have to recognize there is a deliberate policy from Rome not to favor the relationship between a bishop and his priests. Archbishop Lipscomb was the last Jadot bishop [as the Vatican's apostolic delegate to the United States from 1973 to 1980, Archbishop Jean Jadot was largely responsible for the selection of American bishops]. What was characteristic of those bishops was [that] they were local pastoral leaders, and they enjoyed the support of their [priests]. There were exceptions . . . who came from outside, but the vast majority were local pastoral leaders who enjoyed a relationship with their priests. And they weren't going someplace else.
>
> And currently, I would say—I counted it one time—that out of one hundred bishops appointed, maybe five or ten are from the diocese to which they are appointed. And the general understanding is if they are young enough, they are not staying. So the deliberate policy [is] to make sure that the relation-

ship is between the bishop and Rome, rather than the bishop and the local priesthood. We really have to recognize it clearly—it was a deliberate policy. Just as the Jadot policy was a deliberate policy, because back at that time there was a strain developing between the bishop and the priest, [when there were efforts] to organize a union of priests in California and the like. And it was a specific policy by Rome to try to strengthen the relationship between bishops and priests.

Murnion's comments offer the standard account of the differences between Archbishop Jadot and his successors. If the contrast can be overstated (for instance, under Archbishop [now Cardinal] Pio Laghi, Jadot's immediate successor, more pastors and fewer chancery officials were appointed bishops than under Jadot),[2] it remains true that the percentage of bishops who headed dioceses where they had been ordained priests dropped significantly after Jadot's departure; the move was away from local leaders, in favor of other characteristics.

Criticism of the methods of selection of bishops, it seems, is something around which the entire church can unite! Self-identified liberals and conservatives find common ground in criticizing the general narrowness of the consultation process: the laity have virtually no voice; priests have minimal voice; and even many bishops have little voice, as one of the conference participants who was a bishop indicated. By way of contrast, John Strynkowski, who served at the Congregation for Bishops for most of Archbishop Jadot's tenure as apostolic delegate, noted that Jadot was "scrupulous" about consulting broadly on the local level.

In recent years many of the men chosen to be bishops have had personal connections to the American cardinals who sit on the Vatican's Congregation for Bishops. The point is not that such nominees are necessarily unqualified but that the selection process unnecessarily restricts the kinds of men chosen. That process, several participants from across the ideological spectrum agreed, seeks and finds good, "safe" men. Liberals and conservatives disagree, naturally, on what the opposite of "safe" entails. More conservative Catholics, having strong reservations about the so-called Jadot bishops and their alleged doctrinal wobbliness and bureaucratic leadership, would desire bishops willing to teach hard, uncomfortable doctrines and to confront church and culture when necessary. More liberal Catholics, lamenting top-down leadership and the primacy of litmus tests on what they consider to be secondary teachings such as birth control, would press for a non-clericalist, collaborative style of leadership able to foster the gifts of priests and laity alike. Despite these large differences, most would agree the process needs to be fixed, and the conference participants who spoke on the topic expressed a desire for bishops to be local and permanent, when possible. Distance can sometimes be helpful, particularly if a diocese or a presbyterate is divided, but an outside nomination should be the exception. A bishop needs to be close to his priests and people, even—or especially—if he needs to challenge or correct them, and that closeness is possible only on the basis of a sustained familiarity.

Such closeness is complicated, as we have seen, by the unequal relationship of priests and their bishop. Having already examined this strain from the bishop's perspective, we now turn to the priest's perspective.

At the conference, Donald Cozzens described the "schizophrenia" that can result from the priest being, in the words of Vatican II (*Lumen gentium*, 28; *Christus Dominus*, 16; *Presbyterorum ordinis*, 7), both a "son" and a "brother" to his bishop:

> In many dioceses, the bishop insists that priests refer to him by his ecclesiastical title. Perhaps that's part of temperament, perhaps that's respect for the office, but I think it's a very complicated relationship, and I think we're far from finding a comfortable way of relating to our bishops so we can appropriately support them and they can support us. There seems to be a kind of schizophrenia here. They are father to sons and then elder brother to younger brothers. And we are trying to pull it off at the same time and to say it's both. We also have a kind of feudal system going on. I think at one time the priest for the most part came from a working-class family. And we became working-class princes once we were ordained. Well, that seems a little exaggerated, so working-class vassals. Then maybe working-class serfs.
>
> . . . I find it tricky relating to people who are in authority over me where their nod and their judgment is all-important. There's no criteria of performance in terms of assignment or promotions, so if we want to get ahead we have to be thought well of in the eyes of the bishop, and that puts the priest into a situation where I think it's hard to be an adult.

This balancing of the priest's sonship and brotherhood is more of an art than a science, more a matter of wisdom than of technique, as Dennis Sheehan's aforementioned comments on the priest–bishop relationship suggested. Surely, many relationships face the same problem as does the priest–bishop one—how do leadership and friendship cohere?—but that latter relationship takes on a greater intensity because of celibacy and obedience: a priest's life is literally in the hands of his bishop—in the rite of priestly ordination the ordinand places his hands in the bishop's and promises obedience to him and his successors—in a manner unequalled in other relationships and workplaces. This dependence—for assignments, personal and professional validation, even financial support—can be life-giving or crippling.

Perhaps a way forward can be seen in the writings of the late Herbert McCabe, an English Dominican who specialized in Aquinas. In "God," an essay from his collection *God Still Matters*, McCabe notes that, for Christianity, the opposite of "adult" is not "child," but "servant." A servant, he notes, may be treated very well by the master, but never belongs to the family; he or she remains fundamentally unequal. Sonship or childhood, on the other hand, implies a genuine equality: the father remains the father and the son the son, surely, but their love involves equality, a full sharing of life, rather than even the most benevolent and generous inequality of servanthood. The "glorious freedom of the children of God," of which Paul wrote in Galatians, is possible only in the love that brings equality. In this precise sense, the good bishop, while remaining a true father to his priests, invites his priests to leave behind a crippling dependence and to embrace the freedom of real equality. And, as McCabe points out, the father (the bishop) must give his children (the priests) the necessary space to be themselves rather than projections of his control.[3] That the relationship between a priest and his bishop often falls short of such loving equality does not deny its validity or necessity.

Less theologically, there comes a time, too, when one must stop blaming one's literal or figurative parents for one's problems in life. Their influence—good and bad—shapes us decisively, but we also remain free to rise above—or surrender to—those problems. Thus, if a priest resents being passed over for a desirable pastorate or the episcopacy, he must have the maturity to deal with such anger or disappointment, take it to prayer, and see how he can best serve God in the task at hand. To do otherwise is to surrender, as Donald Cozzens puts it in *The Changing Face of the Priesthood*, to the dysfunction that keeps one trapped in adolescent, even infantile behavior, far removed from adulthood and personal integrity.

I want to conclude this section with two suggestions by conference participants for improving the priest–bishop relationship. Several participants criticized an overall lack of candor in the church—priestly numbers and vocations were particularly sore topics among some priests, who felt that some bishops were unduly optimistic about the future or unwilling to allow any discussion of the topic. One way forward is the model of the marriage encounter, suggested by Dennis Sheehan:

> [M]aybe we've come to the conclusion that in the United States, bishops and priests really need to go on a marriage encounter. And I'm serious about that. That particular structure of critical discussion is something which it would appear anyway that the typical American priest and the typical American

bishop are not terribly good at. And the question that our discussion raises in my mind is, what do we need to facilitate that kind of conversation? We've all talked about the priest's integrity and adulthood, and what have you, but we have not talked about perhaps putting in place the kind of conversation, the kind of structured conversation that would lead beyond the lack of adulthood and lack of integrity that seems to characterize a lot of the relationship between priests and bishops. I mean, I am particularly struck because I deal in counseling pre-marriage couples, [and] I always raise with them: how do you fight? But it never occurred to me that one of the aspects of priesthood is our inability to fight with each other. And I point out to [engaged couples] that a good marriage relationship involves knowing how to fight and come out of the other end with an agreement, but frankly it never struck me that this is not a skill we teach priests in the seminary.

More important still for the priest–bishop relationship is the need for forgiveness. In the midst of the challenges sketched in this chapter, none of which will ever be fully met short of the eschaton, it is important to remember, as Patricia Kelly noted, that progress won't be made apart from the demanding practice of Christian forgiveness:

I think we have to get into being very concrete about living the life of forgiveness and reconciliation. It's one thing to be mad at your bishop. You know, I've been mad at people over my lifetime. And it's one thing to be mad at your presbyterate. It's one thing to be mad at anybody. But when we hold onto that stuff, and when it develops isolation, it is totally contrary to what we claim we are and what we're called to. And it has devastating effects. So we may disagree—that's fine, to reverently and appropriately disagree—but we are called to love one another and we are called to invite one another into reconciliation and forgiveness—even if that's not an immediate thing, if it takes a long time. That has to be part of the redemptive imagination that we consider normative.

Priests

Priests face increasing tensions not only in their relationship to their bishop but also to their brother priests. In *Evolving Visions of the Priesthood*, Dean Hoge and Jacqueline Wenger reported that while priests report high levels of personal support from family (59 percent reported "strong support"), nonpriest friends (50 percent), staff members in ministry (49 percent), and parishioners (43 percent), they find significantly less satisfaction in their relationships with fellow priests (29 percent); only bishops (24 percent), the Vatican (13 percent), and national organizations such as the USCCB and the National Federation of Priests' Councils (2 percent) ranked lower in terms of support. Hoge's and Wenger's findings were confirmed by the conference discussions. I was struck above all by the consensus that emerged on two themes: the isolation and the competition experienced by many priests in their relationships with one another.

Isolation is simply an unavoidable part of the human condition. That isolation is compounded for priests, however, by the increasing distances—geographical, generational, ideological, and theological—that separate them from their brothers in the presbyterate. Philip Murnion, as recorded in this chapter's epigraph, spoke of the demoralization caused by a lack of a common mission in the presbyterate and the church as a whole; too often, priests are left on their own to construct their own ministry and spirituality. One priest in *Evolving Visions of the Priesthood* likewise said that parishes in his archdiocese were increasingly "owner-operated" franchises, operating without a "full-blown mission or a vision." The lack of a common vision may be due to several factors. One, raised at the conference by Donald Wolf, is the breakdown of intergenerational priestly solidarity. Priests today, he finds, no longer tell the stories of older and deceased priests—those giants and dwarfs of past years—that he heard when he was ordained over twenty years ago: "And so, not only are we alone in our parishes to face the onslaught of new issues and new concerns, [and] unconnected to each other [now]—with the pastor across the street, or down the block—but [we're also] unconnected with those who have ministered in the past to bring the church to where it is now."

A second cause, possibly related to the first, is the continuing reception of Vatican II and its attendant difficulties. Priests, like everyone else in the church, differ over the meaning of the council and its implications for the church's life today. What, for instance, does evangelization entail? What is the mission of the laity in the church and in the world, and how is it best fostered? What is the relationship between worship and justice? How ought the church engage the broader world? These questions and others don't admit of a single answer, and many legitimate, faithful answers may stand in tension with one another. In my own archdiocese of St. Paul-Minneapolis, for instance, the archdiocesan-wide evangelization initiative seeks to develop believers' personal relationships with Jesus and to support work for social justice. Both goals are constitutive of the church's mission, certainly, but most believers will incline toward one or the other and argue for its priority. "What can we give to others," the "evangelical" says, "if we aren't intimately bound to Jesus?" "How can you say you love Jesus," the "activist" replies, "if you don't love and serve your brother or sister in need?" And, when such differences arise, they are often difficult to resolve harmoniously. There is a reason why such disagreement is called *odium theologicum*, and it is no surprise that priests are afflicted by the same polarization that afflicts the entire church. It is hard to have a common mission when the church is divided in many ways over the purpose and meaning of its most significant event since the Council of Trent.

A further irony, of course, is that many of the priests who desire greater priestly solidarity would likely resist or even resent any attempts by the bishop or the diocese to foster it. My sense is that, sometimes, many priests would like to have it both ways: deeper communal mission and greater personal and parochial independence. Priests, again like everyone else in the church, can find it hard to let go of their personal preferences for the sake of a common mission.

Underlying these experiences of isolation are the difficulties that priests encounter in forming and sustaining genuine friendships. If, as Andrew Greeley writes (reporting on the doctoral research of the priest Thomas Nestor), priests actually report "significantly higher levels of intimacy in their relationships than other men" and are more likely to offer support and nurturance, they nonetheless face the same challenges as do most men in American culture.[4] Gerald Fogarty framed this issue in the different communicative styles of men and women:

> I think when we are talking about friendship between priests, we have to look at friendships between men. Everybody cites Deborah Tannen, but most people haven't read her. But it's very interesting to read her about the difference in communication between men and women. A number of years ago, I had this close woman friend of mine with her children. We put the kids to bed and this other Jesuit came in and started talking. She was staying in a Jesuit community that had extra guest rooms. And I kept trying to include her in the conversation. And she wasn't helping me, and finally she said, "I found this fascinating. It's the first time I've seen you in a typical male conversation, where you talk about things and not yourself." And I think of that often. I notice with female students, they'll come in and ask me, "Where were you raised? How many sisters and brothers do you have?" And so forth. [Whereas t]he male species is the Alpha Wolf. They are trying to see if they can get the best of me.

This generically "male" difficulty is compounded by particularly priestly and religious modes of relationships. William Morell, an Oblate of Mary Immaculate, offered a striking account of his experiences in seminary and in community:

I was in the seminary at a time when [the prohibition against] "particular friendships" was in vogue. We had the same rule, that if you stepped across the threshold of a brother's room you might as well pack your bag and get out. . . . But I honestly think formation in those days was absolutely backwards. The one thing you feared the most was having a best friend in the seminary, and you avoided it at all costs. And if you happened to have a best friend, you hid it as well as you possibly could.

When I got out, I found out the one thing a priest needs more than anything else in the priesthood is a brother priest who is a friend—not his counselor, not his spiritual director—a friend. I lived in a community where we had four guys leave the priesthood and one guy arrested for pedophilia and thrown in prison for ten years. I didn't know any of that. I lived across the hall; I lived with these people. I didn't know any of that. I mean, it doesn't seem possible. And when I was hauled into court, they said, "How is that possible? How could you not know? You're a brother priest, you lived in the same place, how could you not know?" I wanted to tell them to look around. This is the condition. It is unbelievable.

As Morell indicates, communities of priests—be they diocesan or religious—can sometimes be little more than dormitories, whose residents lead separate lives and eat together only occasionally. In such environments, friendship and accountability can go by the wayside, thereby leading to resignations and criminal activity. Jeremiah Boland spoke honestly of priests' complicity in these kinds of failures:

There's a lot of finger pointing of priests at bishops. But if priests are honest, we have not been too swift when it comes to due diligence in regards to one another. I suspect there isn't a priest in this room that hasn't lived in a situation where we were with someone who we really in fraternity and charity and compassion could have been more honest and helpful to them, and we have had our own avoidance of issues and mishandling of situations.

Beyond the various forms of isolation, priests' relationships with one another are marked by what can be described only as the dark underside of the priesthood: jealousy, envy, competition, ambition, peer pressure. Even though I have had substantial professional and personal interactions with priests, I was surprised at the priest participants' virtual unanimity in this regard. Most laity, I think, are completely unaware of these elements. Archbishop Oscar Lipscomb recalled at the conference the moment when he became aware of that underside:

But let me offer another thing about the competition, the sense of what I can only call "undue ambition," if you want to put it that way, that leads to the sort of clergy faults and flaws that are too much a part of our culture or our caste, if you want to put it that way. The lowest moment I think I had in all of theology took place in either the first or second year in Rome, and we were still taking moral theology. We had a great lecturer, Franz Hürth, a Jesuit who was just fantastic. His name is legendary; he's long since dead. And one day in class he was speaking about the virtues and the vices, and he was talking about envy. And he said, in one of these little couplets that Rome is so famous for, and it left me devastated that day, *Homo homini lupus, sacerdos sacerdoti lupissimus*—"Man is a wolf to other men; a priest is most wolf of all to other priests." And I thought, "What am I getting into?" Because this was not my experience of priests as I had known them as a kid growing up. It certainly wasn't my experience of my contemporaries. Oh, there were some guys that were more about studies and making grades, and things like that, but this wasn't true of most of us, and those who did that kind of thing, we thought they were, pardon the expression, "jerks."

Although Archbishop Lipscomb concluded by noting that in his experience the vast "generality" of priests avoid such extreme behavior, other participants argued that envy and ambition are deep-seated in the priesthood. This competitiveness can start at the very beginning of priestly life, when seminarians begin to sense the various "tracks" for priestly assignments and careers. Mark Hession spoke of his own seminary experience:

I grew up in an interesting internal culture in a seminary in the Northeast [St. John's Seminary in Boston] where we watched with each other for eight years as priests would come in and take a look at candidates, if you will, fellow seminarians. [Coming from the Fall River diocese,] I happened to be an extern in that particular system. We were reminded we weren't part of the local culture. We were externs, interestingly enough, though we were Caucasian and male—but we saw a culture already at work that could be described as it is elsewhere in one of the other [conference] papers as tribal. . . . But fellows would come and take a look at candidates in the first years of college and the first years of theology, seeing who might be future curial officials, seeing who might be future seminary professors, and then, to give a third area, with regard to a sort of pitiful reference, who were going to go to the barrios. There were three categories. And, of course, the first two [groups] might have yielded candidates through the system who eventually make fine bishops, at least in that systemic analysis, and naturally the third one [went] to the barrios, those who would be pastors.

While such tracking is common to many institutions and professions, it is particularly weighty in a celibate and relatively unremunerative priestly culture. Shorn of material wealth or a family of one's own, the priest relies heavily on his ministry for self-worth and validation. That ministry, however, often lacks immediate, tangible results. Priestly culture, moreover, tends to discourage priests from claiming credit for their achievements; self-promotion is not well received. A prestigious pastorate or administrative appointment, not to mention nomination as a monsignor or ordination to the episcopate, can consequently become one of the few visible markers of a priest's achievement and status. And, sometimes, one's disappointment at not being selected for a desirable post is exceeded only by one's anger or envy at a brother priest's success. Donald Cozzens spoke on this point:

We speak of the fraternity of the priesthood, and I think it's more than simply a literary image, it's more than rhetoric, and I think it's even more than a metaphor. I think we priests do relate to each other as brothers—with all of the competition, tension, that goes with working with brothers. I think one of the major faults or sins of the priesthood is envy and competition. I think we priests are slow to affirm a brother priest, congratulate a brother priest, let him know if he's given a great talk or written a great article for the diocesan newspaper. We're rather slow there.

Now, if a brother priest is getting beaten up, then our spirit of fairness surfaces and we reach out to him. But we have a very complex relationship on a psychological level alone, not to mention other levels.

Philip Murnion, while acknowledging the reality of competition in the priesthood, suggested that the deeper pressure was conformity and the desire for acceptance:

It's not so much fear of failure as fear of not being liked. It's also an enormous pressure to fit in, not to stick out. I can remember that in the seminary, because I wound up creating some new things at the seminary, [I felt] enormous pressure from my fellow seminarians until it was successful. And then they were great supporters of you. But before that. . . .

And in general [there is] that notion of fitting in, anybody who sticks out a little bit is somebody that's trying to attract attention to themselves. Most priests, I think, are not ambitious; they want to be liked, but they don't expect themselves to climb in the structure, I think. But they want to be liked. And the best was, one time in 1928 or something like that, the bishop ordaining his priests in New York said to them, "If I don't hear a thing about you for the next fifteen years, I'll know you're doing a good job." Fit in, like a member of the choir whose voice doesn't stick out. And I think that pressure is enormous, to fit into the general pattern, and not to stick your head above water.

The vast majority of priests at the conference had achieved significant public recognition—they were distinguished scholars, seminary rectors, officers at the USCCB, and so on—and so may have felt such competition and peer pressure more keenly than other priests. Yet, Andrew Greeley—himself one of the handful of best-known priests in the United States—has noted that such back-biting and "praise mixed with a knife in the back" is the occupational hazard of the priesthood:

> When a layman mentions to a priest that Father X is a good preacher, the response is likely to be, "Yes, he preaches well, but he doesn't get along with the kids." Or "He's really good, but all he does during the week is prepare his sermon." Or "Everyone says that and it's probably true, but he's not an easy man to live with."[5]

Although the conference took up a wide range of issues surrounding priest–bishop and priest–priest relationships, some topics inevitably did not come up. In light of constant protests of isolation and loss of a corporate mission, I was surprised that no one raised the need for priests—diocesans especially—to forge better fraternity, particularly through new forms of communal living. I was also disappointed that generational differences among priests were almost entirely overlooked, probably because of the conference's lack of seminarians and younger priests (only one priest was under forty-four years of age). Dean Hoge, especially in *The First Five Years of the Priesthood*, has explored these differences, which are indicative of broader differences, even polarizations, affecting the church in the United States. His research confirms what most observers suspect: younger (ages twenty-five to forty-five, as of 2001) priests are closer in attitudes and ecclesiology to older (over sixty-six) priests than to middle-aged (forty-six to sixty-five) ones. They exhibit particularly strong differences over priestly identity and status, which signal equally strong differences over ecclesiology, liturgy, collaboration with the laity, and the meaning of Vatican II. There remains deep disagreement, obviously, over whether these shifts among younger priests are a sign of reversion and restoration or of synthesis and advance, and we will address these questions in this book's conclusion.

Whether the problem be envy or an inordinate desire to fit in, with one's bishop or one's brother priests, the only sufficient response, however, is a deeper conformity in prayer and service to the will of God. This answer may sound like boilerplate, pious rhetoric, but the problems sketched in this chapter, which are as much spiritual as psychological, must receive a spiritual resolution. Yves Congar, who endured immense physical and ecclesial suffering in his life, wrote eloquently about the cost—and fruit—of such fidelity:

My deepest conviction—and by God's grace I have lived and practiced it—is the same as John the Baptist's: "No one can receive anything except what is given him from heaven. . . . He who has the bride is the bridegroom; the friend of the bridegroom, who stands and hears him, rejoices greatly at the bridegroom's voice; therefore, this joy of mine is now full. He must increase, but I must decrease" (John 3:27–30). Each one has his part to play and his own path to follow in the sacred history which God writes. For each one the finest task is the one which has been allotted to him and it is in accomplishing it faithfully that he will be truly great, truly fruitful, and ultimately happy. One must neither belittle nor exaggerate one's part: "My lot has fallen for me in pleasant places; yea, I have a goodly heritage" (Psalm 16:6). A man does not increase his stature by belittling another, by being jealous of his destiny, but rather by laying himself open to what God has given him to be and to accomplish and by corresponding joyfully with it.[6]

Chapter Four

The Priest as Pastor and Person

I remember the very good pastor in my own church, saying that when he was ordained a deacon many years ago at St. John's Seminary in Brighton [Massachusetts], that the ordaining bishop said, "Remember you're not being ordained for your own fat self."

—Thomas O'Donnell

Whether a priest is heterosexual or homosexual, in love or not, it will not drive him to resign unless at the same time he feels lonely or unappreciated. This is a basic finding of our research.

—Dean Hoge, *The First Five Years of Priesthood: A Study of Newly Ordained Catholic Priests*

In the first decade or two after Vatican II, the word "co-responsibility" was often used to describe the full, active participation of all members of the church in its life and mission. Cardinal Leo Josef Suenens, the Belgian archbishop who was one of the council's architects and who helped popularize the concept, particularly hoped that the laity would assume their rightful dignity in, and responsibility for, the church. If the word itself has fallen into disuse over the years, and if some conceptions of co-responsibility inadequately respected the church's divinely willed hierarchical structure, the vision nonetheless remains pressing. Commentators from across the ideological spectrum, for instance, united in their conviction that the clerical sexual-abuse crisis revealed the need for the laity to take—or be allowed to take—greater responsibilities and initiatives in the church; the scandals exposed all too painfully the bad fruits of clericalism and lay marginalization. Many priests—whom Andrew Greeley calls the "lower clergy," in distinction to bishops and cardinals—have similarly desired greater voice in the church and to be treated as adults, rather than as vassals.

The journey to adulthood is not always easy, though, and it is rarely linear. The ongoing reception of Vatican II gives abundant proof of the advances and stumblings on that road. Priests, who are called to be "men of communion," can find themselves struggling to foster that communion with the laity, the bishops, and themselves. Many of the conference participants spoke of the challenges posed to priests by an increasingly adult laity and by their own call to maturity. Several speakers noted signs of growing adulthood among the laity— the changing status and roles of women in church and society, for instance, or the increasing number of lay ecclesial ministers and the consequent need for collaborative ministry—and the need for priests to develop attendant skills such as friendship, listening, and persuasive leadership. Others spoke of the priest's call to adulthood, one fostered in seminary and continuing formation, as well as in his intimate, celibate friendships with priests and laity alike. For both laity and priests, the summons to adulthood is central, as the church's life depends on all believers rising "to maturity, to the measure of the full stature of Christ" (Ephesians 4:13).

Laity

In contrast to the often critical, if constructive, tone of the conference's discussions on priests' relationships with their bishops and fellow priests, talk of the priest's relationships with the laity was strongly positive on the whole, focusing more on challenges than on critiques. Two sets of challenges came to the fore. The first set concerned the aforementioned changes in relationships brought about by the increasing adulthood of the laity. The second involved the skills needed to foster those relationships, such as friendship and listening. Several participants mentioned, too, that the priest–laity relationship should be a mutual, two-way one, in which both parties help form each other.

The roots of these challenges can be traced back over decades and centuries. Some are more theological, as in Vatican II's renewed emphasis—after centuries of neglect—on the laity's equal dignity and responsibilities in the church and the world. Others are more sociological and historical. Gerald Fogarty's conference paper on relationships among priests, bishops, and laity in American Catholic history, for one, recounted the growth of the Catholic Church in America from a largely immigrant, laboring-class community to an educated, middle-class one. This shift has similarly affected priests: where they once were "among the best educated men in a predominantly ethnic community in the city," Fogarty wrote, "most priests now serve ethnically mixed parishes in the suburbs."

As a result of these shifts, both priests and laity have found themselves adjusting to new identities and roles. Archbishop

Daniel Pilarczyk of Cincinnati, chair of the Initiative, described the change in priestly identity in recent decades as

> the shift from the priest as member of a caste or as nobleman, to the priest as servant leader whose task is to help lay people be lay people. I think when I went to seminary in 1948 as a high school sophomore, priests were special, they were different, they were "up there." And if you were lucky enough to get through the seminary, you could get "up there," too. Nobody ever said that, but that was the way it was then.

While priests are still accorded by most laity a certain respect and deference on account of their ordination, the Archbishop rightly noted that they no longer occupy the pedestal that they once did. Priests have had to adapt to no longer being the most educated members of their parishes or receiving the largely unquestioned acceptance of their authority. So, too, have they moved from being effectively the sole ministers in their parishes, to being leaders of collaborative ministry— a point to which we will return. Corresponding to this new image of the priest as servant-leader is the emergent adulthood of the laity. Donald Cozzens noted that these two developments go hand-in-hand:

> Part of the new context is that the individuals to whom the priest is ministering are becoming adults. I think you can speak of the people of God for a rather long time, assuming the attitude of passive acceptance of what is given to them by their spiritual parents [the clergy]. So as the Catholic adults, whether they are

well-informed theologically or spiritually or not, become psychologically adults vis-à-vis their place in the church, the context changes. . . . But I think this new context is different today in the sense that on almost every level of the church people now are beginning to think as adults; they are very eager to serve the gospel and the mission of the church, but as adults. And to be a servant-leader in this new context is quite a challenge. First of all, it means the servant-leader has to truly be an adult. And the servant-leader then has to lead other adults. That interaction can be profoundly challenging, and I think it is quite new overall.

But, what does adulthood mean in the church? Although numerous participants raised the theme, no one developed it in any detail. Most likely it meant that believers—be they laity or "lower clergy"—should be active subjects of the church's life and mission, rather than passive objects who merely follow orders or receive services. Adulthood thus involves some measure of activity and initiative, commitment and responsibility, but it takes any number of forms and practices that affect the church's mission and that can conflict with each other. These variations have significant implications for priestly ministry.

Think, for instance, of the differing visions of adulthood proposed by Paul Lakeland and Pope Benedict. Lakeland, a British-born Catholic theologian who teaches at Fairfield University, argues in *The Liberation of the Laity: In Search of an Accountable Church* that the Catholic laity have been oppressed by a centuries-long, nonbiblical separation between the laity and clergy. Too often treated as children or as sheep by the clergy, the laity must name their oppression and move from being objects of the church's mission to its primary subjects: "Infantilization. Conscientization. Self-definition. These are the Egypt, Sinai, and promised land of lay liberation." The result of the laity's liberation, Lakeland holds, will be an adult church marked by structures of accountability, participation, and consent, as well as a world more profoundly humanized.

Pope Benedict, for his part, sees adulthood as the believer's full stature or maturity in Christ. Lost in the media frenzy over his criticism of the "dictatorship of relativism" in his homily on the morning of the conclave's opening, was his call for an adult faith that is "deeply rooted in friendship with Christ." Reflecting on Ephesians 4 and John 15, the then-Cardinal Ratzinger said that such adult friendship involves a complete sharing of one's life and will with Christ, and that it alone enables one to resist the ideologies and fads that keep one trapped in a willful, impetuous adolescence. Unanchored from deep familiarity with Christ, the believer has "no criterion by which to distinguish the true from the false, and deceit from truth."

Both men call for an adult faith, then, but emphasize different aspects of it. Lakeland speaks more in "structural" terms, Benedict in "spiritual" ones. One calls for activism, the other for intimacy. While I judge Pope Benedict's vision of Christian adulthood to be more substantial and compelling in its Christocentrism, it remains that both his and Lakeland's understandings lay significant responsibilities on both laity and clergy. For Lakeland, the laity can no longer accept the deadening, familiar comfort of a passive consumption of ecclesial services and goods, while priests must renounce clerical privilege and see their primary task as supporting the laity in their work to transform the world. For Benedict, the laity are called into a demanding, liberating encounter with Christ, in which his life becomes their own; clergy, in turn, must have a "holy restlessness" in guiding their people to a faith capable of resisting the "ideological currents" that militate against Christian life.

A key task for the church and particularly its priests will be discerning, in the midst of these and other visions, how best to foster adulthood among the laity. Calls for hierarchical accountability and structural reform cannot be dismissed out of hand as the tired whinings of liberal Catholics, for they are concrete ways in which the equal dignity and responsibility of the laity are manifested. And, conversely, it is sobering to realize, as Gerald Fogarty said during the conference, that the best-educated laity in the church's history is often woefully ignorant about its faith. Any discussion of adulthood in the church, I submit, must acknowledge the empirical and pastoral reality of the often weak catechetical formation of children, young adults, and even many adults. Priests, as the leaders of their people, need to find ways of ministering to a laity that is at once increasingly adult and immature.

A key role in that ministry is played by those who have become known as lay ecclesial ministers (LEMs). This somewhat inelegant, even bureaucratic, phrase describes those who work at least twenty hours a week in salaried church ministries such as religious education and youth ministry. The vast majority of laity, of course, live out their Christian vocation in the world. Vatican II spoke of the "secular" character that is proper to the laity (*Lumen gentium*, 31; *Apostolicam actuosi-*

tatem, 2, 7), and, as we saw in chapter 1, Cardinal George of Chicago has claimed that the greatest shortcoming of the postconciliar church has been its failure to form a laity capable of engaging and transforming the world in light of the gospel. An adult Christian, in this view, is one whose daily, "secular" life is shaped from beginning to end by faith and who, in turn, seeks to make Christ present in the world.

Nonetheless, this "secular" dimension of lay life is complemented by the "ecclesial." It is only in the last few decades, after centuries of constriction, that ministry in the Catholic Church has expanded beyond priesthood. The renewal of the permanent diaconate has certainly contributed to such growth, but greater still is the explosion of lay ministry. LEMs in the United States have increased from 21,569 in 1990 to 30,632 in 2005, and for nearly a decade they have outnumbered parish priests. This growth affects not only the substance of church ministry, but also its style. Priests are no longer effectively the sole ministers in the parish, and they have had to adjust—some willingly, some less so—to the new situation. Ann Lin, a member of the Initiative's advisory committee and an associate professor of public policy and political science at the University of Michigan, recalled a conversation at the conference:

> This [situation] might be best characterized by what Father [Francis] Kelley said to us last night about being in a parish where someone finally asked him: "Well, what do you do?" and he said, "I don't do anything, you've found my secret." We talked about this as the collaborative leader. It was a phrase that came up a lot yesterday. The collaborative leader's job is to

enable the ministries of the laity and of the other ministers in the parish—but primarily, because there are more laity than other ministers, the ministries of the laity. It is also to sponsor, provide, enable spirituality or spiritual development, and this can come from the people, too. This can come from popular religiosity, popular movements, popular devotions. It can certainly come from lay people leading prayer, or enabling prayer. But, again, the model that we talked about when we talked about the parish, is the model of the priest as the collaborative leader, as the priest who eventually in some sense disappears so that other people can do the ministry.

Such "disappearing"—which was meant positively, in terms of the priest as one whose ministry gives rise to a host of other ministries and services—can nonetheless give rise to fears that lay ministry undercuts the distinctiveness of priestly ministry (the laicization of the clergy) and contributes to the creation of a new elite in the church (the clericalization of the laity). These concerns, expressed in such documents as the Vatican's 1997 "Instruction on Certain Questions Regarding Collaboration of the Non-Ordained Faithful in the Sacred Ministry of the Priest" and *Christifideles laici*, Pope John Paul II's 1988 apostolic exhortation on the laity, account for much of the resistance to lay ecclesial ministry. At the November 2005 meeting of the USCCB, for instance, several bishops objected to terminology used in "Co-Workers in the Vineyard of the Lord," a proposed document on lay ecclesial ministry. They argued that the terms "ministry" and "minister" should be limited solely to the ordained or to those who exercise a stable, established office in the church. Cardinal Avery Dulles, whose public support for the terminology of LEM at that meeting helped secure the document's passage over such objections, later expanded on these themes in a March 2006 lecture at Fordham University. Noting that numerous church documents from several popes and the American bishops have applied "minister" and "ministry" to the laity, he argued against competitive, zero-sum conceptions of the clergy–laity relationship or of the secular and ecclesial dimensions of lay life. He held instead that, at a time of growing secularism and of a laity in increasing need of formation in prayer and doctrine, the collaborative ministerial work of the laity and the clergy could only further the church's mission of evangelization and transformation of the world. Lay ministers, in particular, have an irreplaceable role in staffing Catholic schools and parishes, supporting Catholic families in their various responsibilities and challenges, and helping Catholic businesspeople and other professionals integrate their faith and work. In such ways, ordained ministry, lay ministry, and lay activity in the world all reinforce one another.[1]

Whether accepted grudgingly as a stop-gap measure in response to declining number of priests or gratefully as a gift that fosters the talents of all the baptized, the growth of lay ecclesial ministry ensures that ministry in the American church, at least, will be collaborative ministry. The ecclesiological and theological tensions that attend to collaboration, though, are accompanied by pastoral and sociological ones. Dennis Sheehan, for example, noted that both the laity and lay ministers can have contradictory impulses about collaborative ministry. They are often eager, on the one hand, to participate in church leadership and ministry and can be critical of priests who restrict such opportunities. On the other, they sometimes revert to clericalism or paternalism, in which they overemphasize priestly authority: "Father," Sheehan dramatized, "get the bishop out/keep him in, say something for/against the war in Iraq." Sometimes, in an adolescent manner, they yearn for independence and yet can regress to a Father-knows-best mentality. Such growing pains are perhaps inevitable as the church responds to the increasing adulthood of its members.

Moreover, much sociological data indicates the existence of significant tensions between younger priests and LEMs, particularly those who are older and/or female. Dean Hoge and Jacqueline Wenger have written in *Evolving Visions of the Priesthood* that these conflicts center on "status, ministerial domain, and turf more than on creedal or theological issues."[2] Touching on such matters as the nature of the differences between the ordained and baptismal priesthoods, these disagreements are particularly strong among lay ministers with higher levels of education. Younger priests, Hoge and Wenger reported, are often perceived by lay ministers as conservative, intent on preserving a sense of priestly distinctiveness, unsupportive of lay ministry, poor listeners—especially to women—and nonconsultative. The same lay ministers, though, noted that these priests tend to have more life experience and better management skills than many older priests. It is interesting to note that while tensions in worldviews between younger priests and younger laity will likely grow in coming years (contrary to the broad claims in such works as Colleen Carroll Campbell's *The New Faithful: Why Young Adults Are Embracing Christian Orthodoxy*, younger Catholics on the whole are more liberal than their predecessors), younger lay ministers, like their priest peers, tend to the more conservative; how this generational situation will affect church life and ministry is unknown.

It has become a commonplace—depending on one's stance—to lament or to celebrate younger priests' supposed conservatism. While it is true that they often have a sharper sense of priestly distinctiveness than their middle-aged brothers in the presbyterate, that sense of identity need not translate into clericalism or triumphalism. As less than a handful of the conference participants were under forty, a final comment on this topic will come from a lay minister quoted in *Evolving Visions of the Priesthood*:

> The new priests perceive themselves as clergy first and foremost. They are conscious of their status as priests. However, they are very service-oriented and they see the laity as partners. They are glad to have laity work alongside them. They are not as clerical as their immediate predecessors, that is, those ordained in the last ten years of the 80s. There is a wide acceptance of the trends of the Second Vatican Council among the new priests. There is an excellent degree of tolerance of the views of others—but with some notable exceptions. They focus on the hierarchical aspect of the church and would rather not have the laity come too close to the altar.[3]

It is imperative that, in a time of polarization in the church, younger priests be allowed to develop their own identity and not be forced into generational and theological stereotypes. For example, Andrew Greeley, whose work I admire greatly, sometimes fails in this regard, unable to see in the former Cardinal Ratzinger or in present-day seminarians and newly ordained much else besides restorationist impulses and a renewed clericalism; he conflates, unnecessarily and unfairly, priestly distinctiveness and priestly superiority. Faced with such dismissals, those priests and seminarians who are already suspicious of more liberal Catholics will only find further cause to harden their own identity—something that seems to happen already in some seminaries, where conservative seminarians and liberal professors push each other to ideological extremes—while those who are less defensive will find this stereotyping insulting. Either way, polemics will do nothing to advance the collaborative ministry that the church needs today.

The call to adulthood and the rise of collaborative ministry point to another dimension in priest–laity relationships: the changing status of women in the church and in society. Women in the United States are better educated, have greater professional opportunities, and represent a more vocal, public presence than ever. In *The Church Women Want*, a book growing out of a series of dialogues sponsored in 2000–2001 by the Initiative, a predominantly liberal group of Catholic women reflected on the impact of these and other changes on Catholicism, taking up such themes as embodiment and its implications for male and female identity, ethnic and racial diversity among women and in the church, and women as "leaven" in the church and in society. Two contributors give a sense of their labors. Elizabeth Johnson, a member of Initiative's advisory committee, argued that women, as full images of God and embodiments of Christ, ought to be allowed to represent Christ as ordained ministers; anything less denies their equal dignity and relegates them to subordination. Mary Ann Glendon, another member of the advisory committee, focused more on "secular" concerns than did Johnson. She wrote of the witness or "leaven" that women of faith can offer to the world: a distinctively Christian feminism that affirms women's dignity as it challenges dominant cultural patterns of parenthood and professional life. A common theme among most of the contributors was the need for women to be involved more deeply in ecclesial leadership and decision-making—matters related, but not reducible, to priestly ordination.

The emergence of lay ministry raises these concerns in a new way. While women have always formed the backbone of the church's day-to-day life in parishes, schools, and hospitals, they have now become ministers to an unprecedented degree: 80 percent of lay ecclesial ministers are women. A quick glance, for instance, at virtually any parish bulletin reveals the overwhelmingly female character of church ministry. As parishes become increasingly communities with only one priest, the pastor is sometimes the only male on the parish staff. Kenneth Woodward, a contributing editor at *Newsweek*, has noted that, from Sunday night to Sunday morning, the parish is almost a wholly female world.[4] These changes—from a time when ministers were male and clerical to one where the majority are female and lay—naturally have an impact on the priesthood today.

Although the conference participants in San Antonio spoke about the priest–women relationship less than might have been expected, several important themes cropped up. The first was the particular qualities and desires that women bring to the church. Sharon Euart sketched a portrait that placed relationality at the heart of women's hopes for priestly ministry:

> A couple of years ago I was asked to speak to seminarians at a theological college on "What do women expect from their parish priest?" I realized that I couldn't speak for all women, first of all, but I did want to respond in a way that could be helpful to the seminarians. So I surveyed a group of women, about 50 to 60 women, a cross section of ages, ethnic backgrounds, lay and religious. And in my discussion with the seminarians I shared with them the responses to the two questions I asked the women: "What do you expect from their parish priest?" and "What was the most memorable experience you had in relation to a parish priest?"
>
> . . . Some of the major expectations that these women had—they were all Catholic and pretty active in their parishes—[were] a willingness to listen, a respect for others, being present for important occasions in their lives and the lives of their families, spiritual nourishment. Many of them did say in the very beginning that they would want their parish priest to be a holy, spiritual man. So I think that is a very significant piece. Other expectations they had were: a priest who would seek their opinion; one who would acknowledge their presence in the parish community; and one who would utilize their gifts and their experience and allow them to participate in some decision-making in the church. Liturgy and the quality of preaching were much farther down than the personal

interrelationship that develops. . . . Granted, this was a small group, but I do believe it is indicative of what we might find in large populations.

While women's expectations of priests are obviously not monolithic, Euart's findings are supported by what David DeLambo, in *Lay Parish Ministers: A Study of Emerging Leadership*, has called the "feminine dimension" of lay ministry and, I would add, of lay life. This feminine aspect, he argues on the basis of a national survey of over one thousand lay ministers and pastors, emphasizes "relational experiences" such as staff prayer, working retreats, and faith-sharing, while the masculine favors "task-centered activities like staff-meetings"; it privileges being-together over doing-together. His research also confirmed the sense of some conference participants that while priests often feel they relate well to women, women can be less positive about that relationship. Pastors, he notes, tend to characterize their relationships with lay ministers as a "team," while the lay ministers describe it as "staff." These relationships, however, are overwhelmingly characterized by both groups as "respectful" and "professional."[5]

Building on Euart's comments, a few speakers stated that women sometimes find it hard to work collaboratively with younger priests, but no one explored whether those difficulties are because of differences of sex, ecclesiology, or other factors. Andrew Greeley's research even suggests that, contrary to some stereotypes, younger priests on average have higher regard for women than do older ones.[6] These relational difficulties, though, are a two-way street. Doris Gottemoeller, R.S.M., the senior vice-president for mission and values integration at Catholic Healthcare Partners and a former president of the Leadership Conference of Women Religious, noted that priests at times find their ministry and identity questioned by some strands of feminism:

> One of the aberrations of a certain kind of feminism is to devalue the priesthood because currently only males are ordained. And so you see at times a kind of dismissal of priests, particularly in a liturgical setting, and pushing them to the side, because, after all, it is a role restricted to men. I see priests play into that, as well.

In sum, the increasing adulthood of the laity—among the baptized in general, and among women and lay ministers in particular—poses a number of challenges and opportunities for priests and for the church.

We look now at some of the virtues and skills—friendship, leadership through listening and speaking, and the mutual formation of priests and laity—needed to foster that adulthood in the laity and in priests themselves.

A number of conference participants identified friendship as the foundation of healthy, adult priest–laity relationships. Adulthood and friendship go hand-in-hand. Friendship, Aquinas held, involves a communication or sharing of love. This love, which is the very life of God, brings about a certain equality, as when Jesus tells his disciples that he calls them friends, not servants or slaves, for he shares with them everything he has received from the Father. In this sense, adult relationships call for the equality of friendship. Several participants, priests and laity alike, spoke of the importance of intimate lay friendships as a key to priestly happiness and as an antidote to clericalism. Dennis Sheehan spoke of the ability of the priest retaining his identity as a priest to enter into real friendships with people who are the baptized laity or who aren't Catholic at all—real friendships, not just parochial, official kinds of relationships. Real friends who are lay people, not who neglect you as a priest (that's not what I would ever want to have to happen) but who can deal with your humanity as well as your priesthood, and with whom you can relax the way you can relax with your family.

Such friendships with laity were sometimes disapproved of in the past, as priests were encouraged to socialize with other priests. I find helpful here the example of John Paul II and the decisive role played in his life and ministry by his friendship with *Środowisko* ("milieu"), a group of about two hundred men and women who gathered with him—whom they called *Wujek* ("uncle"), even as pope—and one another for prayer, study, and recreation. Over decades, he baptized their babies, skied and hiked with them, and discussed their intellectual and spiritual concerns—a depth of intimacy that was rare for a priest of his time, when clerical friendships were the norm. He even learned of his appointment as an auxiliary bishop of Kraków while on their annual two-week kayaking trip.[7] From these friendships he deepened from the inside his understanding of the laity.

A growing problem today, though, is that the depth and breadth of lay friendships that John Paul enjoyed—up through the end of his life—are now achieved with greater difficulty, because of the prevalence of "circuit-rider" priests spread thin by overwork. Ann Lin noted at the conference the cruel irony that, because of the priest shortage, the priest's sacramental responsibilities often separate him from his people:

> I always feel that coming to these conferences from the Midwest is so different than coming from the East Coast, where the priest shortage is there but it hasn't hit in the same ways. Coming from the Midwest, where you do have shortages of priests, where you have circuit-rider priests, etc., one of the things you see is the priest who is able to fulfill only the sacramental role, or who is needed primarily to fulfill that sacramental role that only the priest can fill. This has therefore isolated the priest from so many other things happening in the community because he simply doesn't have time or space or the knowledge of his parish, when he is so busy only conducting and baptizing and he is going to several different parishes to do that. So, how do we understand that sacramental role of the priest and how it sometimes ends up separating the priest from the community, rather than anchoring the priest within the community?

This distancing is particularly destructive for priests, because they report such high levels of personal support from the laity and find some of their greatest joys in serving them. In these circumstances, the priest is reduced, as Susan Wood noted in her conference paper, to a sacramental dispenser and an ecclesial administrator, unable to be the pastor and the presence his people need. If the priest is called to be a "man of communion" par excellence, how painful must that distance from his people be. He suffers the loss of intimacy—doubly wounding because of his celibacy—and his people lose their intimacy with him. The bond between priest and people—the Johannine vision of the Good Shepherd who knows his flock and whose flock knows him—is wounded, with predictable results for the lives of priests, their people, and the entire church. When combined with weakening bonds of clerical friendships, these losses can be devastating for priests.

If friendship, according to Aquinas, involves communication, then good priest–laity relationships surely involve both listening and speaking. Donald Cozzens offered helpful distinctions between types of listening:

> In light of trying to teach listening skills in our seminaries, it's dawned on me that we priests, and I think the bishops [at the conference] might agree with this, we have been consciously or unconsciously trained to listen for questions, since we are the priest-minister, so that we might answer the questions clearly in light of Catholic teaching; and secondly, we've been trained to listen for problems so we might offer a pastoral response. Those two forms of listening are integral to the life of the priest. In addition, though, to listening for questions and problems, I do not think priests and bishops have learned how to listen to be both informed and transformed. There's a different kind of listening that's necessary, especially in the church today. And if we clergy tend to listen as the answer person, or as the problem-solver, we're not going to listen in such a way that we can be both informed and transformed, and in the process converted.

Building upon Cozzens's remarks, Patricia Kelly spoke of Jesus' "redemptive listening" to the adulterous woman and to the woman at the well, a listening that goes beyond "questions" and "problems" to drawing out the other's deepest identity and desires. Such listening, as Jesus demonstrates, avoids both acquiescence and condemnation in bringing about conversion. One thinks also of the *Rule of Benedict*'s counsel to listen with the "ear of the heart," with the core of one's being. And, sometimes, attentive presence is the only, and the greatest, gift the priest can offer to his people. The following passage from William Faulkner's *A Requiem for a Nun* will resonate with any priest:

> Somebody to talk to, as we all seem to need, want, have to have, not to converse with you nor even agree with you, but just keep quiet and listen. Which is all that people really want, really need; I mean, to behave themselves, keep out of one another's hair; the maladjustments which they tell us breed the arsonists and rapists and murderers and thieves and the rest of all the anti-social enemies, are not really maladjustments but simply because the embryonic murderers and thieves didn't have anybody to listen to them: which is an idea the Catholic Church discovered two thousand years ago only it just didn't carry it far enough or maybe it was too busy being the Church to have time to bother with man, or maybe it wasn't the Church's fault at all but simply because it had to deal with human beings and maybe if the world was just populated with a kind of creature half of which were dumb,

couldn't do anything but listen, couldn't even escape from having to listen to the other half, there wouldn't even be any war.

The priest must also speak, though, and nowhere does he do so more publicly or significantly than from the pulpit (or other places in the church, as wireless microphones—if not liturgical law—allow!). I was disappointed that, while many conference participants alluded to preaching and their often frustrated desires for better homilies, no one spoke about it at any length. I want therefore to highlight some "outside" contributions to the topic.

No one in the American church has spoken more effectively or witheringly about the state of priestly preaching than Andrew Greeley. It is, he writes, the number one topic of laity's conversations about priests, and this layperson can only agree with him. Only 18 percent of Catholic laity, however, consider their clergy to be "excellent" preachers, compared to 36 percent of Protestant laity. Greeley argues that while some priests have greater gifts for preaching, all priests can develop the talents they have. Since preaching requires creativity, "[n]o one should be ordained who has not done some kind of creative exercise—a short story, a cycle of poems, an art or photo exhibit." "This is not a joke," he adds in a footnote. Priests, he continues, should be able, within a few years after ordination, to speak without notes—just like the laity do in their workplaces. If a priest "needs psychotherapy or public-speaking training to preach well, then so be it. Let him get the training before ordination."[8]

In the same address to the National Catholic Educational Association in which he took up the theme of the seminarian's personal conversion to Christ, Dennis Sheehan said that while seminary homiletics programs have improved overall, priestly preaching has not. Apologizing to his audience for aping Andrew Greeley, he made two suggestions for better preaching, one practical and the other spiritual. First, (future) preachers need to develop clarity and coherence in thought and expression. Too many homilies in his view are abstract, wandering, overly autobiographical, unable to develop artfully an image or a theme. Seminaries must make the measurement of clarity and organization a part of every evaluation at every stage of formation and be willing "to tell a bishop that his seminarian simply cannot think clearly and speak straight enough to qualify him for the pulpit." If singing ability is required for ordination in some Orthodox churches, Sheehan suggested that demonstrated preaching ability should be necessary for ordination to the Catholic priesthood.

Second, seminarians and priests must immerse themselves in scripture, so that its worldview becomes their own and they see the world through its lenses. He recounted the tale of the young man who went to the rabbi to tell him of his desire to become a rabbi. The rabbi told him simply, "Go and read Torah." The young man returned months later, saying "Rebbe, I have been through Torah ten times." And the Rabbi told him, "Go back now and read Torah again. It is not enough that you go through Torah. You are not ready until Torah goes through you." This assimilation, Sheehan noted, is a matter more of conversion than of technique, but it must be fostered in the seminary if future priests are to become better preachers of the Word.[9]

The difficulties that Sheehan mentions arise in part, I think, because seminarians today often come from business or technical backgrounds. They thus often lack the exposure to the liberal arts, and especially the humanities, that previous generations of seminarians had as a matter of course. This is not to say that those generations were marked by humanistic excellence, but rather that they received some training in working with texts and images, rather than in developing quantitative skills—however helpful they may be. The priest who does not read or appreciate the arts will simply lack the creativity needed to preach well, and his ministry to an adult laity will suffer.[10]

Friendship and its expression in listening and speaking point, moreover, to the mutual character of the priest–laity relationship. The most heated discussion of the conference, as chapter 2 recounted, involved the theme of the priest as icon of Christ, and one of the central points of contention was the degree to which priests and laity form each other. Paul Griffiths, for instance, argued that the priest is an icon of Christ whose calling is to form laity so that they can transform the world; his comments on the priest–laity relationship, necessarily brief because of the conference's format, tended toward the unidirectional: Christ → priest → laity → world. John Strynkowski, by contrast, proposed a more bidirectional model:

> I appreciate very much the notion of icon applied to the priest. I would say, first, that every icon, like every symbol, is capable of many different meanings and therefore we can't confine the significance of the icon to simply one thing. I would be a little bit troubled, though, in understanding that the priest simply forms the people and seeks their conformity to

Christ. There is truth to that, but I think that as a priest myself, I've been formed by the people, too—people whom I serve. As I've gotten to know people in parishes, and for many years my assignments were simply weekend assignments, but as I got to know the people over the years, I would always be very humbled before celebrating Mass on a weekend, looking out—maybe from the back of the church—looking out at the congregation, and knowing the stories of almost everybody in that church, and recognizing how they are living the paschal mystery. And it humbles me in the sense that what I am going to be doing now in celebrating the Eucharist and in preaching, I have to do very, very, very well, because these people, so many of them are truly on the Cross. A friend of mine once said that behind every family there's a mess. Whatever I do in that Eucharist, I want to make sure that they go home strengthened and nourished for what they have to face for the rest of the week.

So the formation is reciprocal. Christ is there. I can't speak about the whole church, whether it's half-Christian, half-pagan, or what. But in terms of my experience, in terms of the people who come to Eucharist on Sunday, I would say there is a lot of Christ present at the Sunday Eucharist and in the people who come.

Strynkowski's comments were well received by the other participants and serve as a caution against a too-easy dismissal of the laity as a "half-pagan" bunch corrupted by a decadent world—an appealing temptation when one's ministry seems barren or irrelevant. Such paganism does exist, clearly, but it does so alongside real and often deep faith.

The mutuality involved in adult relationships, however, can make leadership difficult, as seen in the tensions faced in the priest–bishop relationship, where bishops are called to be both fathers and brothers to their priests. The priest's leadership of an adult community, like the bishop's of a presbyterate, relies more on persuasion than on command. Even though the Catholic Church considers itself to be the divinely willed, ordinary means of salvation, it remains that believers enter and remain in it voluntarily. Leadership of the community, then, must always respect that voluntariness and treat members as adults. I know, for instance, that my wife and I relate differently to each other and to our children; the sometimes summary direction of our children we exercise as parents differs from the consensus building and give-and-take that we practice as spouses; "Because I say so" works (sometimes) for subordinates, not partners. Genuine authority might be seen best as invitation, rather than as control—even if the latter is necessary at times.

It remains, though, that the priest is charged with forming his people. The all-too-real dangers of clericalism and authoritarianism should not give rise to an abdication of pastoral leadership. The servant-leader, as William Morell noted, must lead, after all, and cannot settle for being a mere moderator for his community. Persuasive leadership, it seems to me, embraces not only dialogue and consensus but also the persuasion of holiness. The priest's own holiness and witness of life are his most persuasive means of leadership—not least in a time of crisis provoked by the priestly and episcopal failings of the sexual-abuse crisis. Pope Paul VI, in his apostolic exhortation *Evangelii nuntiandi*, said that "modern man listens to witnesses more than to teachers, and if he does listen to teachers, it is because they are witnesses" (41). In this sense, Griffiths's conception of the priest's iconicity, despite its incompleteness, has the merit of recalling the priest's irreplaceable role in forming and leading the community in holiness.

Since only a handful of voices at the conference emphasized these responsibilities, I turn to a recent address by Archbishop Charles Chaput of Denver, which offered a perspective complementary—but not competitive—to Strynkowski's. Speaking to a group of Philadelphia priests, he said that the first thing the church needs from its priests is that "the priest [be] unavoidably a leader; not a facilitator or a coordinator of 'dialogue,' but a leader of faith. . . . Even in an age of the laity, priests set the tone of Catholic life." He then quoted St. Francis de Sales on the relationship of priest and people: "Holy priest, devout people. Devout priest, honest people. Honest priest, sinful people." The archbishop, I think, was arguing not for a renewed clericalism or a two-tiered theology of Christian holiness, but rather a recognition that priests, as the visible, sacramental leaders of their communities, "set the tone." It is undeniable that lay holiness and activity can flourish despite poor priestly leadership, but it is equally undeniable that good priestly leadership catalyzes the entire community.

Priests, he continued, must also "help [their] people convert—even if they don't want it," and also "need to understand the fabric of [their] people's lives—without losing [their] zeal to transform it, and them." Listening must be complemented by teaching and guiding. Treating laity as adults also means challenging them and holding them to high standards.[11]

The priest, then, has the duty of leading and of forming his people. Sometimes that involves listening, sometimes speaking; sometimes it involves learning, sometimes teaching. It takes real wisdom to know when to do each. Howard Bleichner offers a helpful analogy: newly ordained priests "often resemble golfers with only two clubs in their bag, a driver and a putter. They are either heavy-handed in their use of authority or they abdicate, avoiding its exercise. Only with time do priests learn to use the full range of clubs at their disposal."[12] The adult priest requires wisdom in knowing how to minister to and lead an adult laity, and that wisdom transforms both his people and himself.

The Priest Himself

The priest's pastoral wisdom and capacity for communion depends greatly on the shape of his own self, his own humanity. In *Pastores dabo vobis*, Pope John Paul II wrote that the priest's human formation—his capacities for relationship, love, freedom, conscience—is the basis of his spiritual, intellectual, and pastoral formation. While called to minister in the name and person of Christ, the priest does so only as a human being among men and women of every kind. Lacking a mature, healthy humanity, the priest will falter in his ministry and become an "obstacle" to Christ (43). John Paul II's words echo the Letter to the Hebrews' vision of the priest as one who "had to become like his brothers and sisters in every respect, so that he might be a merciful and faithful high priest in the service of God" (2:17).

The conference did not address the priest's relation to self as extensively as it did his relationships with Christ, his bishop and brother priests, and the laity. Discussion was slated for the final session on Saturday afternoon (Sunday morning was devoted to summary and evaluation), but themes from previous sessions spilled over into that slot. In the compressed time available, though, the participants offered much on the priest's interior communion, particularly as expressed in his celibacy.

The priest's call to adulthood involves a call to personal integrity and wholeness. His life should be of a piece, transparent and simple to all who encounter him. Reality is often more complicated, of course, and the effects of a priest's fragmentation and immaturity can be tragic. Ann Lin, who was a social worker at Covenant House in New York City and a member of its residential faith community, spoke of Bruce Ritter, its Franciscan priest–founder:

> Who knows why, but the other thing [besides his success with Covenant House], of course, that happened to him, is that in his success he stopped living in community, and he—in my understanding from people who knew him—did not have the time to pray and to enrich his life, to enrich his relationship with God. He was eventually accused of having sexual relations with some of the young men who came to the shelter and, though he denied [these accusations] vehemently, there was quite a bit of evidence that it was in fact true. He was forced to step down in a scandal that

hurt the shelter, that system he built tremendously, and of course that also hurt him and hurt a lot of people who had a lot of faith in him. . . .

I bring this story up because we are talking about a priest's icon and idol relationship to God, a priest working in the world, a priest praying, as if they were all separate things, and you've got to choose one or the other of them. And, in fact, in Bruce Ritter's case they all worked together, some at the very same time. When he was having these relationships with these young men, he was also leading people to Christ; he was also helping people; he was also hurting people— and certainly hurting himself and his relationship with God.

God holds them together in a mystery that our arguing about the categories that they fit into can't penetrate. And the useful thing for us to do is in some sense not to argue whether the priest should be more one or more the other, but to say the priest functions as [them all]. We cannot keep the priest from being an icon, we cannot keep the priest from being an idol, we cannot keep the priest from seeing his job as some-times to work in the world, and we cannot keep the priest from seeing his job as being what brings others to God and inspires them to go out and be called to the world. And since we cannot keep these things from happening, what we need to do is figure out how to support the priest and to teach the priest to support himself through enriching his relationship with Christ.

Patricia Kelly addressed this internal fracturing by speaking of the priest's "*communio* within" and its implications for the priest and his ministry:

Somebody brought up the notion of *communio* earlier, and what concerns me is the absence of *communio* within. This is the absence of the kind of self-competence (and that sounds very psychological and I don't mean it in that way), the kind of comfort that comes from having a clear sense of who I am, and what I've been called to do: the distinctiveness of role and the distinctiveness of priesthood. Part of what gets in the way of this conversion, or even the redemptive imagination, is that [as a psychologist] I hear so many priests talk about why they don't trust the hierarchy, or why they don't trust their bishop, or don't trust whomever, whomever, whomever. And because they don't feel they have a forum, or they are unwilling to take the risks to find a forum, it remains unreconciled, and it turns into bitterness, and people make contracts of compromise. In other words, they say, "I'm going to keep my nose down, I'm going to do my job in my parish. I'm here at St. Somebody, and this is what I'm going to do." The universality of the church [is ignored], and the reality of holding on to that bitterness serves as a cancer throughout that person, even though it's unnamed, it's unrealized, it's hidden.

In other words, there are a whole lot of inequities that are never named. Obviously we have had 18 months of headlines about some of those, but those are not the only ones. I mean there are all kinds of inequities of power, inequities of affirmation, inequities of conciliation, inequities of commitment. This is in the background coming from a culture that is commitment-challenged to begin with. So what happens, then, is people have to accommodate by learning how to be dissociative, and that dissociativeness becomes a way of survival and has incredible consequences in terms of robbing people of their creativity, of their faithfulness, of their sense of hope, and their redemptive imagination.

The priest, like any other person, cannot compartmentalize for long their lives. Such bracketing or segregation may work for a time, but it will catch up with the priest—whether dramatically, as with Bruce Ritter, or subtly through the inner dissipation that corrupts the outer witness of his life and ministry.

A key aspect of this "*communio* within" is the priest's celibacy. Because more ink has been spilled and computer keys tapped on celibacy than on virtually any other dimension of the Catholic priesthood, I want to focus on a handful of points raised by the conference participants. One topic that will not be discussed is the church's discipline of mandatory priestly celibacy. There are solid arguments for changing the church's discipline (e.g., the centrality of the Eucharist to Catholic life; the life and familial experiences brought to priestly ministry by married men; the issues raised by the priestly ordination of married Protestant ministers received into full communion with the Catholic Church), and there are weak ones (e.g., that celibacy is inherently pathological or inhuman, that changing the discipline will increase vocations). So, too, are there strong and weak arguments for maintaining the long-standing discipline. But, optional celibacy for diocesan priests was not discussed at the conference—not because it was suppressed but because the participants focused on more foundational issues, to which we now turn.

Celibacy, in the first place, must be understood not as a hatred of sexuality but as a way of loving and relating. This is an obvious, but necessary, point, for celibacy is often seen—and sometimes experienced—as a legalistic imposition on the part of the church. It is true that the puritanical dimensions of celibacy—the belief, for example, that sexual intercourse renders even a lawfully married priest unclean for sacramental ministry—have been emphasized more than the affective at various points in the church's history; Cyprian Davis, a Benedictine monk and church historian at St. Meinrad School of Theology, presented a paper, "Development of the Theology of Chastity and Priesthood: Mandatory Celibacy for Priests in the Early Church and at the Beginning of the Middle Ages," that offered a fair-minded historical perspective on the topic. Enda McDonagh, an emeritus professor of moral theology and canon law at Maynooth Seminary in Ireland, spoke at the conference of the positive basis for celibacy:

> I think we do get a bit bogged down in the discussion about celibacy in relation to the diocesan priesthood. But we have to remember that, as we've been reminded, it is a value. But like all human values, I think what kills many young people and many priests is that it's taken to be simply a restriction. And, in fact, it's a call to a love-life, a very difficult love-life. And it's a love-

life that's going to be a bit erratic in the course of your trying to realize its value, because you'll be too unloving, or maybe too foolishly loving, sometimes. It is a process. You become celibate as, indeed, I think you become chaste in the course of your life. You're not simply born chaste or born celibate. You know, we used to think we were born chaste and kind of gradually lost it as we went through puberty, or whatever. Until we are sexually awakened we can't be chaste, anyway. And until we're sexually alive and alert and loving, we can't be celibate either, mind you. So it is a long struggle.

Second, if celibacy is about intimacy and relationship rather than avoidance or repression, then it isn't possible without a deep intimacy with the person—and not simply the program or the cause—of Christ. Celibacy is christocentric or it is nothing. This is the single most important thing to be said about celibacy. Whatever practical benefits it may have for priestly ministry—a theoretically greater availability and mobility for ministry because of the lack of familial commitments, the economic reality that a single man is easier to support than a family—celibacy is ultimately about one's love for Christ.

Now, the rhetoric of celibacy can be—and is—summarily dismissed as spiritualist, ethereal, obfuscating. And that dismissal is frequently justified, as much of the language used in the past and even the present does not distinguish itself by its honesty, logic, or simple humanity. It is clear, of course, that celibacy is not essential to the Catholic priesthood and that both married laypeople and the small number of married

Catholic priests can love Christ fully and with undivided hearts. Celibacy, though, bears an irreplaceable witness to the primacy of Christ and his kingdom in one's life and in the world. And priestly celibacy bears an irreplaceable witness that all of our human, created loves will find their fullness only in the heavenly banquet, of which the Eucharist is the sacrament.[13] Cletus Kiley made this point in speaking about the contemporary context for celibacy:

> In order to live celibacy effectively, it seems to me that we need three things: we need a rationale; we need skills; and we need a supportive environment. In the past I think the rationale that was probably given to most people was that it was a higher life. . . . The major skill used was repression. And the supportive environment was a faith community that thought this was a value and rewarded those who did it faithfully and shunned those who didn't. So it was an environment that supported this calling.
>
> The rationale, I think, in the culture we live in is blurred at times. It's not understood or appreciated. There are many more skills needed to live celibacy effectively besides repression. It just isn't enough. And the supportive environment, I think we can understand, does not exist. I don't think it exists in this country in any case. An example in point: In October [2002] there was a description in the *New York Times*, trying to describe Opus Dei; it was around the [canonization] ceremonies for the founder of Opus Dei. But the remark that stood out to me [was that] they described the followers of Opus Dei as engaging in

eccentric practices such as celibacy and lashing themselves with whips—pretty clear [evidence] that the environment is not supportive of one's choice.

Not too long ago, a member of the [USCCB's] National Review Board said, in a discussion about what they thought might be some of the causes of the sexual abuse crisis, "Well, the simple version is people didn't keep their vows." And another of the members of the board—and I thought this was very touching—said, "I think it was a failure of the imagination, that priests have a beloved. A lot of times, though, they can't imagine that, and they have forgotten it, and things get distorted." Well, I thought, he was grappling with the rationale for celibacy. And I think he was on to something.

If not a comprehensive account of the sexual-abuse crisis, Kiley's comment underscored the only sustainable rationale for celibacy: that "imagination for the beloved," Jesus Christ, who is the source of one's life as a believer and a priest. At the heart of every human person is the desire to love and be loved, and the essence of love is to give oneself entirely in service and wonder to another person, be it through marriage, friendship, or celibacy. In a distinctive way, the celibate priest gives himself wholly, in good times and in bad, to the One who loves him first. Divorced from such love for the person of Christ, celibacy devolves into mere pragmatism at best, and workaholism, substance abuse, emotional coldness, and the confirmed bachelor's avoidance of the demands of marriage and family, at worst.

Celibacy is thus a way of loving Christ and neighbor, but,

like marriage, it poses distinctive challenges to those called to it. Several participants drew a distinction between loneliness—which is part of the human condition, as any married person can attest—and isolation, which contradicts the call to communion at the core of every person. The relational abilities of priests are at least as good as other men's, but the challenge remains for priests to develop healthy relationships with all kinds of people in and outside of the church. The increasingly isolated living arrangements of priests, diocesans especially, are an enormous problem for the priesthood and the entire church. It is not good that man be alone, of course, or that a priest live alone in a rectory, separated from his brother priests and unaccountable to anyone—clergy or laity—for his daily routine.

Celibacy, moreover, is a way of relationality that should go beyond sexuality to embrace everything that the priest does and is. It calls him to an ascesis that touches the roots of his being. Peter Casarella offered a profound insight on this point:

> I want to say one word about chastity, recognizing fully that chastity is something that we all—single, married, religious, and priests—are all called to. But I think chastity in many ways is a kind of foundation for the sexual celibate as well. And I define chastity here in the terms of the hymn in Philippians 2, "Christ Jesus, though he was in the form of God, did not regard equality with God something to be grasped." I think the fundamental element of chastity here is the "not grasping." The grasping in question is not just or primarily sexual, it involves ambition, jealousy, an

unhealthy and particularly male form of competitiveness, and, as Ernie Cortés said, an inordinate desire to be liked.

Third, Robert Silva, a priest of the Stockton, California diocese and the then-president of the National Federation of Priests' Councils, noted that celibacy, like marriage, is a call to life, and that the priest celibate needs to have deep friendships with women if his celibacy is to be life-giving:

> [A person I know] found out that he could have a soul partner who was a male, a friend, there in the seminary, but he missed what the feminine soul partner gave him. And he asked himself, "Does celibacy mean that I have to give up the feminine? Can I have present to me, deep in my own experience, someone of the other gender as my soul partner?" My response to him would be yes, and it's an extremely important yes, because if he's going to be a good priest he's going to need to know what it means to be a man, and if he's going to know what it means to be a man and masculine, he's got to understand that the feminine in him has to be touched somehow. And the only way he understands more deeply his masculinity is when he is in a relationship with femininity.

I would add that a priest's mother does not suffice for these purposes. Dean Hoge has noted that Catholic seminarians "disproportionately have dominant mothers,"[14] and I have been struck, in my friendships and other interactions with priests, how few of them talk at any length about their fathers.

142

This may be because fathers generally die at younger ages than mothers, as well as to the disproportionate number of priests who are adult children of alcoholics and so may have grown up distant from a parent, especially a father.[15] I wonder, though, how much of that maternal closeness is attributable to the celibate male's need for the feminine. It might also be that a candidate's decision to become a celibate priest is attributable to the strong feminine connection he already enjoys with his mother; celibacy might pose less of a challenge or a renunciation for him than for one who lacks that strong feminine presence in his life. A priest's closeness with his mother is not inherently pathological, certainly, but it is important that he form and sustain healthy, chaste friendships with other women, too.

Fourth, priestly celibacy also raises the issue of homosexuality. The conference, it should be recalled, took place nearly three years before the November 2005 release of the Congregation for Catholic Education's Instruction on the admission of men with homosexual tendencies to seminaries and Holy Orders, so there was no discussion of the suitability of such men for priestly ordination. What did come up, though, was the difficulty that the sexual-abuse crisis raised for the priest's friendships with other priests. Older priests will recall the strictures in the seminary against "particular friendships." One participant said that even putting one foot in another seminarian's room was grounds for expulsion, while another mentioned the rule for walks on seminary property: "Always three [seminarians], never two."

Today, the priest's need for close friendships with other priests can run smack into the need to address the existence of gay subcultures in the priesthood. None of the participants offered a way forward, but William Morell, who had spoken previously about the need for priestly friendship, had this to say:

> It seems to me that the saddest thing happening in the presbyterate these days and in seminaries is this issue of homosexuality, because there is a suspicion for all close friendships that build. And I hate to say it, but it's true. I've heard it, and maybe many of you have heard it. The good friends, I just wonder what's going on. So the one chance that there was for salvation with a brother priest is looked on suspiciously. It's a terrible tragedy.

"Affective maturity" is a phrase often used in ecclesiastical documents to describe matters of sexuality. Its meaning is fairly elastic, ranging from specific matters of sexual orientation and behavior to a broader concern for a person's ability to love freely and responsibly. Becoming a "man of communion" requires of the priest a daunting level of maturity. He is called at once to rise to his full stature in Christ and to help his people rise to theirs. In his Letter to the Ephesians, the apostle Paul writes: "But speaking the truth in love, we must grow up in every way into him who is the head, into Christ, from whom the whole body, joined and knit together by every ligament with which it is equipped, as each part is working properly, promotes the body's growth in building itself up in love" (4:15–16). These words are a consolation to the priest, for they remind him that he is not alone in his life and ministry but stands in communion with the entire church, which is growing toward adulthood in Christ.

The Priest: "Tested in Every Way"

The theology of the priesthood that emerged from Vatican II in the first generation was perhaps not lofty enough to call for heroic sacrifice or to justify the cost of the discipline of celibacy. On this point young priests may be right in their instincts. But an elevated theology of the priesthood will not be found in a return to the theology of the past or by assembling the surface accoutrements of an older era, e.g., birettas, amices, palls. Such gestures speak only of human need, fear, and uncertainty. Such emotions are understandable, but they are not positive enough to chart a course into the future. A loftier theology of the priesthood may yet lie ahead. But it must come on its own as a genuine movement of the spirit. Still, we will be spared no human travail when it arrives.

—Howard Bleichner[1]

In his homily at the Chrism Mass celebrated at St. Peter's Basilica in April 2006, Pope Benedict XVI offered a profound meditation on hands. Hands, he reflected, symbolize human agency, the ability to do and to make, to dispose of the world as one sees fit. In priestly ordination, these hands are anointed and become a sign of the human "capacity to give, of creativity in molding the world with love." Making himself vulnerable, Christ gives himself over into human hands in a special way through priesthood: "The Lord makes us his friends: he entrusts everything to us; he entrusts himself, so that we can speak with his I *in persona Christi capitis.* ~~What trust! He truly delivered himself into our hands.~~" ~~The priest, in turn, is to entrust himself to Christ's hands.~~ Christ, the pope said, continually takes the priest by the hand, holds him up, carries him forward, when—like Peter telling Jesus, "Go away from me, Lord, for I am a sinful man," after the great catch of fish—he becomes overwhelmed by the Lord's greatness, the scope of the priestly task, and his own insufficiency for it. Benedict imagines Christ telling the priest, "Fear not! I am with you. I do not leave you, do not you leave me!"

In this joining of hands, the priest grows into deeper friendship with Christ. Christ's willing and thinking become his own; the power to act with the "I" of Christ expands to become his identity. He shares in Christ's own "awareness of the misery of sin and all the darkness of the world," and his hands hold the keys of forgiveness that open the door to the Father's house, where there are no servants but only friends.

Consciously or not, the priest lives at the intersection of unworthiness and empowerment marked out by the pope and given enduring expression in the Letter to the Hebrews. Tested in every way, the priest, like Christ, knows weakness and the fragility of the human condition. Made perfect by what he suffers, the priest becomes a source of salvation for his people. Even, perhaps especially, in the unremarkable routines of ordinary life, he lives the paradox of strength and weakness, of intimacy and otherness.

It can be objected that such meditations, whether papal or

scriptural, are abstract and impractical in the face of daily parish life—with its utility bills, bake sales, staff meetings, elementary schools, pastoral visits, and sacramental duties—and the challenges of contemporary culture. Faced with such demands, the overworked priest can regard such reflection as a luxury at best, an escape at worst. The move toward a supposedly greater realism or relevancy, though, carries an even greater threat: the loss of the "one thing necessary." In the Book of Revelation, the risen Christ begins his series of messages to the "seven churches that are in Asia" by scolding the church in Ephesus. After praising their industriousness, patient endurance, and rejection of evildoers and false prophets, he goes on to deliver a stinging rebuke: "But I have this against you, that you have abandoned the love you had at first. Remember then from what you have fallen; repent, and do the works you did at first" (Rev. 2:4–5). Love is the one thing necessary, and the Lord calls the Ephesians to recover the love that was once theirs, the love that led them to respond to him in the spring of their lives. These words, painful as they may be to hear, can strengthen the priest when, like the pilgrim in Dante's *Divine Comedy*, he finds himself in the middle of life's journey, dispirited and searching for new direction and purpose. At a time of severe testing—faced with the residual humiliations of the sexual-abuse crisis and the burdens of diminishing priestly numbers—where else can priests turn but to Christ?

The "loftier" theology of the priesthood mentioned in the epigraph at the beginning of this conclusion will emerge only out of an honest appraisal of the contemporary situation and a vision capacious and substantial enough to inspire people to give their lives to it. Toward the end of a long day of conversation at the conference, Dennis Sheehan noted that "We are not dealing primarily with structural issues. We're dealing with relational issues. And those really fall in the area, not necessarily of clear-headed analysis, but of human wisdom and of religious wisdom brought to bear on them." Building on the conference and the preceding chapters, I hope to offer some such insight, and my concluding reflections will touch on four areas: Christ, church, priesthood, and the practices needed for a renewal of the priesthood. My comments are surely not exhaustive, but I trust that they will be illuminating.

Christ

It will come as no surprise that I believe Christ to be the starting point for any authentic priestly renewal. Robert Imbelli put it simply and directly at the conference: "The defining relationship for every Christian, but for the priest in a particular way, is to Jesus Christ. And if we have never fallen in love with Jesus Christ in a way that is life-changing—and I know that that can't be manufactured, but it has to be fostered in some way—then we have no center." The "imagination for the beloved" that Cletus Kiley mentioned and Imbelli seconded is the only thing that gives the priest strength to fulfill his mission. Pope Benedict has been no less insistent in his claim that Christianity is not about a program or a cause but a person—Jesus Christ. "The faithful expect only one thing from priests," he said during his visit to Poland in May 2006, "that they be specialists in promoting the encounter between man and God."

Cardinal Bernardin's *The Gift of Peace* is likewise a remarkably Christ-centered work. Even as he deals with the most personal and even painful of matters—the false accusation of sexual abuse, the spread of his pancreatic cancer—Christ is the constant point of reference, the one to whom the cardinal returns and finds strength. It is a book that leads one to prayer, because he clearly knows and loves Christ. The Catholic Common Ground Initiative, following his example, has placed Christ at the center of its efforts to "strengthen [the church] for its mission in the new millennium." Structural reforms are necessary to this end, but not sufficient or even primary. The Initiative put it well in its foundational statement, *Called to Be Catholic: Church in a Time of Peril:* "The fresh eyes and changed hearts we need cannot be distilled from guidelines. They emerge in the space created by praise and worship." And, such praise and worship are given to none other than Christ, who, "present in Scripture and sacrament, is central to all that we do; he must always be the measure and not what is measured." Any attempted renewal of the priesthood, let alone the church, will founder if not centered in an encounter with the living person of Christ in word, worship, and service.

Church

Contemporary ecclesial disagreements and controversies are often rooted in disagreements and controversies over the interpretation of Vatican II. The priesthood is no different. Much of the clash between cultic and servant-leader models of the priesthood—which I will address later in the conclusion—is rooted in differences over the theology of priesthood articulated at Vatican II. Some maintain that the conciliar texts gave priority to preaching and proclamation of the Word;

others hold to the centrality of the Eucharist and the other sacraments; and still others argue for the primacy of the pastoral service of the community. And yet another group finds in *Gaudium et spes* a call to a more "secular," worldly priesthood that moves beyond the confines of the church and the priest's traditional charge of teaching, sanctifying, and governing. The conference itself did not discuss the council at any length—apart from some discussion over the council's preference for describing the priest as one who acts "in the person of Christ the head," rather than as "another Christ"—but Anthony Ruff, a Benedictine monk and priest who teaches theology at St. John's University in Collegeville, Minnesota, offered helpful insight into how to understand the council's methods and substance:

> I use these two terms to help me think about [Vatican II]: reversion and reconfiguration. [There are] different ways of going at the whole troubled Catholic history of priesthood. And I think it is troubled—for 2,000 years it is a checkered history, gradually developing, of cultic language, ontological language, mandatory celibacy, and I think the Second Vatican Council looks at that whole checkered history and says, "Let's reconfigure it." They didn't say, "Let's revert to an earlier time when we weren't burdened with cultic and ontological and mandatory celibacy language." So, the Second Vatican Council affirms mandatory celibacy very strongly. It did not reject a cultic notion of the priesthood, it retained it. But, it says it's now a part of a reconfigured whole. . . . It seems to me the Second Vatican Council says we

retain ontological language and we think that's compatible with the dignity of all the laity. The Second Vatican Council says we affirm mandatory celibacy, very strongly, and we believe that's compatible with all Christians being a part of a priestly people. We maintain cultic language of the priesthood and we believe that all the people participate in the Eucharistic sacrifice.

Ruff's comments strike me as spot-on in terms of both the priesthood and the council. The council is too often viewed in the manner of the movie *Pleasantville,* whose black-and-white portrayal of a repressed American community in the 1950s gives way to full Technicolor upon its awakening to the joys of sex, freedom, diversity, and creativity. This kind of a reading makes for a provocative story, but terrible history and distorted reality.

Joseph Komonchak's Common Ground annual lecture in 2003, "Dealing with Diversity and Disagreement: Vatican II and Beyond,"[2] offers a helpful way forward, arguing convincingly that the council cannot be seen as a battle between a liberal majority and a conservative minority (the "Cowboys and Indians" approach), but must take account of the differences that existed within the minority and majority groups. The majority, in particular, was marked by a series of internal tensions (e.g., the priority given to the Incarnation or to the cross, the relationship of faith and reason, the engagement of church and culture) that still mark the church today. One sees, for instance, a reductive, even Manichean hermeneutic at work in the tendentious arguments that popes John Paul II and Benedict XVI are reactionaries trying to undo the work of the council. Ongoing differences over the theology of the priesthood will not be resolved until greater consensus on the meaning of the council is achieved. That consensus, I judge, will not emerge fully until younger generations not personally marked—or, even, scarred—by postconciliar controversies bring to bear their own questions and experiences on the council's legacy. Councils often take decades, even centuries, to be received; Vatican II will be no different.

Conciliar hermeneutics also lie behind much of the conflict over the causes and proposed remedies for the sexual abuse crisis.[3] Arguments over the state of the priesthood are often indicative of deeper arguments over the state of church, the council, and even the culture wars of contemporary American life. "Liberal" commentators tend to attribute the crisis to a mixture of sexual repression and clerical–episcopal arrogance, while "conservative" ones tend to ascribe it to a breakdown in sexual morality and a failure of local bishops to exercise the personal episcopal authority that is properly theirs through ordination. Both sides make frequent appeal to Vatican II in support of their positions.

Such arguments can be insightful and contain elements of truth, but they are often polemical and one-sided. Take, for example, sexual abuse by priests. The John Jay study (2004), commissioned by the American bishops, reported that such abuse peaked—in terms of percentages, if not absolute numbers—in those ordained in the early 1970s; more than 10 percent of those ordained diocesan priests in 1970, for instance, were accused of abuse.[4] The ordinands of the early 1970s, born mostly in the mid-1940s, were largely the product of two intersecting worlds: the preconciliar rigidity of their minor and college seminary programs, and the postconciliar laxity of their major seminary formation. Is it possible that these colliding worlds produced a perfect storm of abuse? When faced with this data, though, ideologically committed commentators settle for reductive analyses—abuse as the product of repression or laxity, rather than some tragic mixture of both—that are used to score points and denigrate opponents. The truth may be less satisfying for polemical purposes, but it has the merit of being true. Why cannot both sides admit truth in the other? The priesthood and the church, especially in the aftermath of the sexual-abuse crisis, will not be renewed apart from such honesty and self-criticism.

The contemporary American church and priesthood will be shaped also by the increasing diversity of its members, locally, nationally, and internationally. Francis Kelley, the pastor of Sacred Heart Church in Boston, said at the conference:

> I'm in probably the most diverse parish in the city of Boston. I have just an enormous mix of people. It has just kept growing apace, and they aren't all poor. There are middle-class as well as new immigrants, and some are upper-income. But the one common bond they all have is they are Catholic. They are very different Catholics from Africa, from South America, and from Boston. But they are all Catholic, and they find that as a common bond. And I'm just paying more and more attention to what that means. Other people must have experienced this from around the country. I know we are not the only people with that situation. But that is a big sea change.

Such diversity requires of priests greater sensitivity to different cultures and practices, to different ways of relating. I recall here the comment of Neil Connolly, the pastor of St. Mary's Church, a largely Hispanic parish on New York's Lower East Side, who noted that the priest should "look" like the people he serves or at least enter into their cultures through a "kenosis" of self-emptying service.

Although held in San Antonio, a symbolic center of Latino Catholicism in the United States, the conference did not sufficiently address these issues, largely because the sexual-abuse crisis took center stage. However, if middle-aged and older priests were formed and ordained in the preconciliar church and then had to adapt—quite willingly on the whole—to life in the postconciliar church, today's priests—young and old alike—will have to adapt to life in a "browner" church, to borrow a term from the writer Richard Rodriguez. Formation and ministry will need to catch up to demography and geography: as the Catholic Church in the United States moves from being predominantly white and northern to being predominantly brown and southern, the church's infrastructure and its human capital will have to adapt. Parishes and schools are closing in the Northeast and the Rust Belt, while dioceses in the South and Southwest cannot build them fast enough, let alone provide the priests necessary to sustain Catholic life. So, too, recent immigrants and such writers as Lamin Sanneh and Philip Jenkins have much to tell us about the potential effects of an increasingly "world" Christianity on the Western church. The growing diversity at all levels of the church will have a significant, often unforeseeable impact on the shape of the priesthood and ministry in general.

Priesthood

Foremost among the needs for a renewed priesthood is a more substantial, compelling sense of priestly identity. Philip Murnion put his finger on the problem, in recounting a priest friend's regret that after twenty-five years of priestly ministry he felt alone, bereft of any communal identity and mission. This lack of a coherent vision, let alone the "lofty" identity proposed by Howard Bleichner, may be somewhat understandable in light of the ecclesial, theological, and cultural dislocations induced by the changes of the past forty years. But, it is urgent that one now be developed. The key task, I judge, will be to articulate a strong sense of priestly identity that is unapologetically distinctive but thoroughly relational. My sense is that many of the priests ordained during the council and in the following decade or two hoped to overcome the clericalism that separated priests from the laity and to develop forms of collaborative ministry that could foster the dignity and gifts of all the baptized. This is the model of the priest as servant-leader. That model and those goals remain entirely necessary, but I suspect that they also have often led to a devaluation—however unintentional—of the distinctive, irreplaceable identity and ministry of the ordained priest in the life of the church. The cliché bears repeating: equality does not mean sameness.

A deeper sense of priestly identity, though, cannot be found in a return to what has become known as the "cultic" model of priesthood, which defines the priest through a narrow, individualistic focus on his powers to confect the Eucharist and to absolve sins. The priest, as the conference participants agreed, is a "man of communion," and his ministry must be understood in a broadly relational, ecclesial context. The cultic model, while legitimately emphasizing the priest's distinctive sacramental role, tends toward clericalism and even quietism.

The way forward, then, will involve overcoming, sociologically and theologically, the cultic-servant-leader dialectic that paralyzes much contemporary reflection on the priesthood. That way of framing the identity question is spent, for it has outlived the usefulness it once had. I propose, instead, that a Eucharistic-centered priesthood is the way forward. If the liturgy is the "source and summit" of all the church's activity, as Vatican II held (*Sacrosanctum concilium,* 10), then any vision of the priesthood must be similarly Eucharistically centered; the council, in fact, states that "the ministry of priests is directed to [the Eucharist] and finds its consummation in it. For their ministration, which begins with the announcement of the Gospel, draws its force and power from the sacrifice of Christ" (*Presbyterorum ordinis,* 1).

This Eucharistic vision is thus not narrowly cultic or individualistic but recapitulates all of creation. The church and its priesthood, Robert Imbelli writes, are called not "to return to Trent, but to advance into the new millennium!" He proposes that the priest's vocation is to lead his people "in Christ's Eucharistic way" through a prayerful Eucharistic celebration that leads the assembly beyond itself into Christ, through the formation of a Eucharistic community marked by a spirituality of communion that welcomes the gifts of others, and through a Eucharistic practice of service to the needy and work for structural transformation.[5] Imbelli's vision resonates with Vatican II's teaching that "no Christian community is built up which does not flow from and hinge on the celebration of the most holy Eucharist. From this all education for the spirit of community must begin" (*Presbyterorum ordinis, 6*).

This vision is a tall order, surely, but it emphasizes both the priest's distinctiveness and the relational, ecclesial nature of his ministry. It might also help forge a rapprochement between what I take to be the complementary visions of priesthood offered at the conference by Paul Griffiths and Philip Murnion. And, I would argue, only such a comprehensive, demanding, and inviting vision can summon the generosity needed to respond to God's call to the priesthood.

"The real cause of the vocation shortage," Andrew Greeley writes, "is the reticence of those who are happy in the priesthood and not excessively burdened by celibacy."[6] It is not the mandatory celibacy decried by the Left, nor any of the "isms" (e.g., relativism, secularism, individualism) lamented by the Right. God's call may be harder to hear because of cultural impediments—recall Cletus Kiley's comment in chapter 4 on the changing rationale, skills, and cultural environment required for chaste celibate living today—but the witness of a happy priestly life can overcome that interference. I would even argue that it is the only thing that can do so. Priestly morale remains very high, even in the aftermath of the sexual-abuse crisis. This story of happy, celibate priests must be told, if the crisis of priestly vocations is to be overcome.

If priests are an unusually happy lot and their people have deep affection for them, as numerous surveys report, then why do reports of a morale crisis exist? Andrew Greeley attributes it to "pluralistic ignorance": priests are personally happy, but think other priests are not; they are satisfied with their own bishops but believe that the episcopate as a whole has failed in its response to the sexual-abuse crisis. He observes that clerical gatherings foster such ignorance through their tendency to the lowest common denominators of "envy, misery, and mediocrity."[7]

Another interpretation, perhaps more troubling, holds that this crisis of morale isn't about the present, but the future. Priests wonder how the church will fulfill its mission as priestly numbers decline and workloads increase. They wonder whether their ministry will have any legs, as it were, or what will happen to the increased numbers of priests living alone in rectories. The "dearth of candor" experienced at all levels of the church, as Philip Murnion commented, does not help matters here. Bishops and priests play a "game of chicken" over celibacy, as Greeley notes, with predictable results for the life of the church.[8]

Morale will be further affected in coming years and decades by the state of priestly fraternity. Dean Hoge's research, as we have seen, has shown that priests are at greatest risk of leaving the priesthood when they feel lonely or underappreciated. It is not hard to imagine that, as priestly numbers dwindle and the remaining priests find themselves stretched by overwork and uprooted by responsibilities for multiple parishes, priestly morale will suffer and resignations increase. Diocesan priests are noted (or notorious) for their independence—many, in fact, chose diocesan life over religious life because of that independence—but a stronger sense of priestly fraternity is needed. Apart from the need for common living quarters, small support-groups that meet for prayer and recreation are essential; *Jesu Caritas* groups offer one such model. The need for community will grow as priestly numbers decline and as newer diocesan priests are increasingly no longer "native" to their dioceses, and thus lack the familial and communal roots that sustain well-being. An increased sense of fraternity—whether through living arrangements or support-groups—can also strengthen priests' sense of accountability in their personal and spiritual lives. The demands placed on priests will only increase in years to come, and, without such support, priests and the church will certainly suffer.

That sense of fraternity must be fostered from the beginning of priestly formation. Initial and continuing formation was not adequately addressed at the conference because of time constraints. Katarina Schuth, O.S.F., who holds the Endowed Chair for the Social Scientific Study of Religion at the University of St. Thomas's St. Paul Seminary School of Divinity, prepared a paper entitled "Vocations, Seminarians, Initial Formation, and Continuing Education/Ongoing Formation for Priests: Some Information and Questions" that built on her previous research. A number of topics were raised during the brief discussion: the relative merits of "free-standing" and "consortium" seminaries, differences in the formation of diocesan and religious seminarians, the need for greater continuing formation, and the changing economics and demographics of seminary education. Doris Gotte-moeller, for instance, suggested that "we could probably gather all of the students into half as many [seminaries] and do as much." Her point was seconded by many participants, not least by some of the participants who had served or were serving as seminary rectors and presidents.

A topic not addressed, but pressing in light of the laity's desire for better preaching, was the role of creativity and imagination in priestly formation and ministry. In this respect, Peter Steinfels recently examined the questionnaire developed for the 2005–2006 Vatican-sponsored visitation of seminaries in the United States.[9] Even though the visitation's immediate focus was on formation for celibacy, he argued that the questionnaire's emphases and omissions revealed a disregard for seminarians' cultural and intellectual formation. "There are no explicit questions about the seminarians' capacities for initiative, creativity, or imaginative and consultative leadership," he wrote, and only two questions out of ninety-six addressed seminarians' intellectual potential—a marked disappointment, considering that recent research estimated that only 10 percent of seminarians are "highly qualified" intellectually, while nearly 40 percent have one or more learning difficulties. And, drawing together the cultural and the intellectual, he wondered:

> Given Pope John Paul II's repeated pleas for the "evangelization of culture," it is surprising that only one question out of 96 explores whether seminarians are "capable of dialoguing, on the intellectual level, with contemporary society." Why not a few further questions like: "Do the seminarians follow current events? Do they read serious fiction and show an appreciation for the arts? Do they display an interest in contemporary science?"

Seminarians and priests have different gifts, of course, and not everyone can be a great homilist or intellectual. They must, however, develop their gifts to the greatest possible degree if they are to be effective ministers of God's own creativity. And, they will likely not do so if their formation regards such matters as luxuries or even dangers. "The split between the Gospel and culture," Paul VI wrote in *Evangelii nuntiandi*, "is without a doubt the drama of our time," and priests play leading roles in healing that wound. Their formation needs to help them do so.

Practices

These Christic, ecclesial, and priestly concerns will bear fruit only to the degree that they are sustained by effective practices. Prayer, as intimacy and friendship with God, is the primary and most important of practices, of course. I suggest, though, three other practices or ways of proceeding that will help renew the priesthood and the church. First is the spirituality of communion, outlined by Pope John Paul II in *Novo millennio ineunte*, his 2001 apostolic letter marking the close of the Jubilee Year in 2000. Noting that the "great challenge" facing the church at the beginning of the new millennium was to make the church "the home and the school of communion," the pope spoke of the spirituality that needed to become the principle of all formation and education in the church, including that of priests. As he described it:

> A spirituality of communion indicates above all the heart's contemplation of the mystery of the Trinity dwelling in us and whose light we must also be able to see shining on the face of brothers and sisters around us. . . . A spirituality of communion implies also the ability to see what is positive in others, to welcome it and prize it as a gift from God: not only as a gift for the brother or sister who has received it directly, but also as a "gift for me." A spirituality of communion means, finally, to know how to "make room" for our

brothers and sisters, bearing "each other's burdens" (Gal. 6:2) and resisting the selfish temptations which constantly beset us and provoke competition, careerism, distrust, and jealousy. (43)

Collegiality and collaboration, the pope noted, are organic expressions of that spirituality. If susceptible to becoming bureaucratic "mechanisms without a soul," they nonetheless are sacramental realities: collegiality is an expression of the bond of sacramental ordination, while collaboration deepens the bond of baptism that unites in equality all believers. The spirituality of communion, the pope concluded, "supplies institutional reality with a soul."

This vision, although not explicitly mentioned during the conference, was echoed by many participants. Time and again the relational dimensions of priesthood came to the fore, whether it be the priest's relationship with Christ, with other clergy, or to his people. John Strynkowski offered some apposite words:

I speak with some trepidation because I'm not a historian, but it just seems to me that we shouldn't privilege ourselves as thinking that we are the first generation to be facing all of these issues. If we go back to the fourth and fifth centuries, for example, just think: the Roman Empire is collapsing, the barbarians are at the gates, the vast majority of people are illiterate, let alone knowing anything about Christianity. Even within the ranks of the church they are still dealing with those who betrayed the church during the persecutions. Many bishops for a period of time seem to have been Arians, so there are many doctrinal controversies. There was also skepticism and a tremendous variety of religions—religions moving in from the East. It was a time of tremendous turmoil. So I think we need to keep in mind that we're not special because we're facing these issues for the first time.

And yet, the church came through all of that. I don't think we should engage in hand-wringing. On the other hand, though, just because it happened before doesn't mean that we can be complacent today. We do have to work through the challenges that are presented to us, but, at that time, one of the things that was significant was the bishops working together in councils, in synods—local provincial synods—a true sense of collegiality and responsibility for the church. And we also had great bishops, such as Ambrose, Augustine, and so on, who provided tremendous leadership for people. Cardinal Newman called the church a noisy factory, so apt, he said, for divine purposes. So in the middle of all the current noise, I think we do have to maintain some confidence and optimism that we do have the resources to come out of this. What they are, I suppose that's going to take a while for us to discover. But, I think that aspect of collegiality, people working together, collaborating, to bring about change—that's going to be important.

In addition to the spirituality of communion, I would also suggest cultivating the practice of paradox. The classical adage states that "virtue stands in the middle," and there is much wisdom in that saying—especially during a time in which the shrillness of the culture wars continues to infect the church's own life. That moderation, though, needs to be complemented by a lively sense of paradox, in which diverse realities are not balanced off against each other as competitors but rather pushed to their respective extremes in a kind of synergy. Decisive leadership and broad consultation, for instance, are often played off against each other in a zero-sum game; many in the church seek to balance the two dimensions like a see-saw (the moderate approach) or to reject one in favor of the other (the partisan approach). Might the way forward, however, involve a paradoxical strengthening of both realities? The *Rule of Benedict*, for example, sets forth a vision of monastic governance in which the abbot exercises Christ's own authority and on serious matters is enjoined to consult all of the community's vowed members, even the youngest. Leadership and consultation reinforce each other, in the *Rule*'s view, rather than compete. To the question "Does the monastery need stronger leadership or more consultation?" the *Rule* answers "both."

Likewise, when faced with the need to recover a distinctive sense of priestly identity and to affirm the adulthood of the laity, the church should emphasize both, rather than see one as a threat to the other—as partisans of all stripes often do. An emphasis on a distinctive priestly identity need not devalue the laity, or vice versa.

Balance and moderation have their rightful place—Benedictine life, after all, is characterized by a life-giving moderation—but my sense is that the church should reject what Richard John Neuhaus has called "Laodicean moderation"[10]—"So, because you are lukewarm, and neither cold nor hot, I am about to spit you out of my mouth" (Rev. 3:16)—in favor of a constructive habit of paradox. The priesthood that the church needs will not emerge from a hesitant balancing act or an angry tug-of-war; neither the moderate nor the partisan hold much brief for paradox. Renewal will arrive only when we are unafraid to affirm the full, distinctive, and relational identities of all states of life in the church. Peter Casarella makes a similar point in holding up the witness of Cardinal Bernardin's life and death:

> The future lies not in liberalism, not in conservatism, and especially not in a fusion of the two. The future lies rather in a diverse set of Catholic spiritual traditions and practices. Cardinal Bernardin, for example, faced his own death as a friend rather than as an occasion for fear. Here we see a favored son of progressive Catholicism reviving the late medieval art of dying well. It seems hard for me to conceive of the late cardinal making an effort to ally his "liberal" self with a long abandoned traditional practice. Wasn't this attitude simply the unitary act of a Christian who confidently hoped to meet the Lord?[11]

Collaboration and paradox lead to a final practice: dialogue. The Common Ground Initiative has placed dialogue at the heart of its work, judging that the church's unity is threatened by polarization and a lack of candor at all levels. The concluding section of *Called to Be Catholic* contains guidelines for constructive dialogue: recall that no person or group in the church is a "saving remnant" over against a corrupt majority; presume the good faith of those with whom one differs; put the best possible interpretation on another's position; and discern the "valid insights and legitimate worries that may underlie even questionable arguments," to list a few. These principles are more easily affirmed than exemplified, but they have borne much fruit in the Initiative's programs—not least in its conference on the priesthood.

In an open letter sent on the day of his death in August 2003 to each of the American bishops, Philip Murnion issued a final call for dialogue in the church. Building on John Paul II's vision in *Novo millennio ineunte* of a spirituality of communion, he invited the bishops to the "deepest discernment of God's will and the widest consultation of God's people," in order to take bold initiatives to address the polarization that, in the wake of the sexual-abuse crisis, had "only grown more acute" since the Initiative's founding in 1996.

But, transformed by his suffering—the last days of which were marked by a transparency of soul apparent to all who visited him—he reached deeper than ever before to articulate a spirituality of dialogue, which is "as demanding in its asceticism as a spirituality of the desert or the cloister." The spirituality of communion, he wrote, calls for dialogue "as its very life-breath: the dialogue of prayer with Jesus Christ, the dialogue of mutual building up on the part of the members of Christ." And, he closed this final letter with the following words that summed up his life's work and his deepest desire for the church:

> Permit me, then, with the last breaths the Spirit gives me, to implore you: Do not be afraid to embrace this spirituality of communion, this "little way" of dialogue with one another, with your priests, with all

God's faithful. Doing so, you will touch not only the hearts of your brothers and sisters; you will draw closer to the very heart of Jesus, the Lord and brother of us all.[12]

The church's common ground, as the Initiative's founding statement affirmed forcefully and eloquently, will be found not in compromise or half-measures or demonization, but in common faithfulness to the Lord: "Jesus Christ, present in Scripture and sacrament, is central to all that we do; he must always be the measure and not what is measured." The Gospel reading at Philip Murnion's funeral was John 12:20–26, which recounts that some Greeks approached Philip (the apostle!) and asked, "Sir, we wish to see Jesus." Philip, together with Andrew, then brought their request to Jesus, who responded, "Very truly, I tell you, unless a grain of wheat falls into the earth and dies, it remains just a single grain; but if it dies, it bears much fruit."

This is *the* Christian paradox: life only through death. Joseph Bernardin and Philip Murnion were priests who, like the great high priest himself, were "tested in every way" by what they suffered, and that suffering has indeed borne much fruit. The San Antonio conference made clear that ours is a difficult but hopeful time to be a Catholic priest. The apostle Paul, in words proclaimed at Philip Murnion's funeral, wrote, "So we do not lose heart. Even though our outer nature is wasting away, our inner nature is being renewed day by day" (2 Cor. 4:16). We ought to have no less courage that such renewal is at work in the church and its priests.

Notes

1 • The Cultural and Ecclesial Contexts of Catholic Priesthood Today

1. Timothy Radcliffe, *I Call You Friends* (London/New York: Continuum, 2001), 67.

2. Cardinal Francis George, "The Laity and the Contemporary Cultural Milieu," *Origins* 33 (September 11, 2003).

3. Dean R. Hoge, William D. Dinges, Mary Johnson, S.N.D. de N., Juan L. Gonzales, Jr., *Young Adult Catholics: Religion in the Culture of Choice* (Notre Dame, IN: University of Notre Dame Press, 2001), 239

4. Cardinal Francis George, "Catholic Higher Education and Ecclesial Communion," *Origins* 28 (February 18, 1999): 609, 611–14.

5. George, "The Laity and the Contemporary Cultural Milieu."

6. Cardinal Francis George, "Address to the Pope," *Origins* 34 (June 10, 2004).

7. George, "The Laity and the Contemporary Cultural Milieu."

8. George, "Address to the Pope."

9. Andrew Greeley, *Priests: A Calling in Crisis* (Chicago: University of Chicago Press, 2004), 131.

10. Andrew Greeley, *The Catholic Revolution: New Wine, Old Wineskins, and the Second Vatican Council* (Berkeley and Los Angeles: University of California Press, 2004). All quotes in the following three paragraphs are drawn from this book.

11. "Why does the word 'evangelization' on the mouths of many clerics seem so unattractive? Why does it sound so often like

high-powered advertising mixed with enthusiastic brainwashing?" (*The Catholic Revolution*, 173).

12. This paper would later appear as the second chapter of Dean Hoge and Jacqueline E. Wenger's *Evolving Visions of the Priesthood* (Collegeville, MN: Liturgical Press, 2003).

13. These data come from Dean Hoge, "The Current State of the Priesthood: Sociological Research." This as-yet-unpublished paper was presented on June 15, 2005, to "The Roman Catholic Priesthood in the 21st Century," a conference sponsored by Boston College's *The Church in the 21st Century Center*.

14. Greeley, *Priests*, 58.

15. Greeley, *Priests*, 131.

16. Greeley, *Priests*, 116.

17. Greeley, *Priests*, 94. It is interesting to note that a recent *National Catholic Reporter* survey (September 30, 2005) of American Catholics indicated that over 90 percent believe that their parish priests do a good job. More than half, however, think that "most priests don't expect laity to be leaders, just followers," and nearly two-thirds agree that their leaders are out of touch with the laity (Mary Gautier, "Lay Catholics Firmly Committed to Parish Life"). While admitting of no definitive answer, the disjunction between Greeley's and the *NCR*'s findings on priestly performance may be attributable to the overall goodwill that believers have toward their priests, despite their dissatisfaction with their actual abilities or performance—much, perhaps, like the relationship of many believers with their church.

2 • The Priest in Relation to Christ

1. Rowan Williams, "The Christian Priest Today." At www.arch bishopofcanterbury.org/sermons_speeches/040528.html.

2. Dennis Sheehan, "Formation for a Holy, Healthy, Effective Priesthood," *Origins* 34 (June 17, 2004): 71–76.

3. Yves Congar, *Dialogue Between Christians*, trans. Philip Loretz, S.J. (Westminster, MD: Newman, 1966), 44–45.

4. Howard P. Bleichner, *View from the Altar: Reflections on the Rapidly Changing Catholic Priesthood* (New York: Crossroad, 2004), 33–35.

3 • The Priest as Presbyter

1. Andrew Greeley, *Priests: A Calling in Crisis* (Chicago: University of Chicago Press, 2004), 122.

2. Thomas J. Reese, "The Laghi Legacy," *America* (June 23, 1990).

3. Herbert McCabe, *God Still Matters* (London/New York: Continuum, 2002), 8.

4. Greeley, *Priests*, 32.

5. Ibid., 107.

6. Yves Congar, *Dialogue Between Christians*, trans. Philip Loretz, S.J. (Westminster, MD: Newman, 1966), 19.

4 • The Priest as Pastor and Person

1. Cardinal Avery Dulles, "Can Laity Properly Be Called 'Ministers'?" *Origins* 35 (April 20, 2006): 725–31.

2. Dean Hoge and Jacqueline Wenger, *Evolving Visions of the Priesthood* (Collegeville, MN: Liturgical Press, 2003), 131.

3. Ibid.

4. Kenneth L. Woodward, "An Unsettled Realm: In Crisis Comes Opportunity," *Boston College Magazine* (Fall 2002). Also available at www.bc.edu/church21/meta-elements/pdf/opening-event.pdf .

5. David DeLambo, *Lay Parish Ministers: A Study of Emerging Leadership* (New York: National Pastoral Life Center, 2005), 147.

6. Andrew Greeley, *Priests: A Calling in Crisis* (Chicago: University of Chicago Press, 2004), 92.

7. George Weigel, *Witness to Hope: The Biography of Pope John Paul II* (New York: Cliff Street Books, 1999), 98–108, 146–47.

8. Greeley, *Priests*, 125.

9. Dennis Sheehan, "Formation for a Holy, Healthy, Effective Priesthood," *Origins* 34 (June 17, 2004): 74–75.

10. For reflections on the importance of the liberal arts to priestly life and ministry, see Bishop Edward Clark, "The Liberal Arts and the Future Priest," *Origins* 35 (August 8, 2005). Bishop Clark, an auxiliary of the Los Angeles archdiocese, writes that higher education has replaced the liberal arts with "technological training," in which students are taught "not to think but to do." Knowledge, technique, and empathy are not enough, he said, but must be rooted in an exposure to breadth of Catholic culture (e.g., art, music, architecture, and literature) and in the development of powers of critical thinking. Only such cultural and critical development enables priests to minister effectively, and to distinguish truth from ideology, reason from emotion, and logic from intuition.

11. Archbishop Charles Chaput, "The Priestly Vocation, 2005: Co-Authoring the Future with God." Available at www.arch den.org/archbishop/docs/12_06_05_thepriestlyvocation.htm.

12. Howard P. Bleichner, *View from the Altar: Reflections on the Rapidly Changing Catholic Priesthood* (New York: Crossroad, 2004), 120.

13. See Robert Barron, "Why Celibacy Makes Sense," *Commonweal* 132 (August 12, 2005): 17–19, at 18–19: "God chooses certain people to be celibate in order to witness to a transcendent form of love, the way that we will love in heaven. In God's realm, we will experience a communion (bodily as well as spiritual) more intense than even the most intense forms of communion here below, and celibates make this truth viscerally real for us now. Just as belief in the Real Presence in the Eucharist fades when unaccompanied by devotional practice, so the belief in the impermanence of created love becomes attenuated in the absence of living embodiments of it. Though one can present practical reasons for it, I believe that celibacy only finally makes sense in this eschatological context. [. . .]

"The appropriateness of linking priesthood and celibacy comes, I think, from the priest's identity as a Eucharistic person. All that a priest is radiates from his unique capacity, acting in the person of Christ, to transform the Eucharistic elements into the body and blood of Jesus. As the center of a rose window anchors and orders all the other elements in the design, so the Eucharistic act of the priest grounds everything else he does, rendering qualitatively distinctive his way of leading, sanctifying, and teaching. The Eucharist is the eschatological act par excellence, for as Paul says, 'every time we eat this bread and drink this cup, we proclaim the death of the Lord until he comes.' To proclaim the Paschal Mystery through the Eucharist is to make present that event by which the new world is opened up to us. It is to make vividly real the transcendent dimension that effectively relativizes (without denying) all the goods of this passing world. And it is therefore fitting that the one who is so intimately conditioned by and related to the Eucharist should be in his form of life an eschatological person. [...]

"People in love do strange things; they pledge eternal fidelity; they write poetry and songs; they defy their families and change their life plans; sometimes they go to their deaths. They tend to be over the top, irrational, confounding to the reasonable people around them. Though we can make a case for it—as I have tried to do—celibacy is finally inexplicable, unnatural, fascinating, for it is a form of life adopted by people in love with Jesus Christ."

Barron's article raised a firestorm of criticism—for its supposedly narrowly cultic conception of the priesthood, denial of the equality of the baptized and the ordained, and denigration of marital commitment—which he addressed (convincingly, in my view) in the "Letters" section of the September 23, 2005, issue of *Commonweal.*

14. Dean R. Hoge, *The First Five Years of the Priesthood: A Study of Newly Ordained Catholic Priests* (Collegeville, MN: Liturgical Press, 2002), 85.

15. Ibid., 83–85.

Conclusion • The Priest: "Tested in Every Way"

1. Howard P. Bleichner, *View from the Altar: Reflections on the Rapidly Changing Catholic Priesthood* (New York: Crossroad, 2004), 213.

2. The lecture may be ordered from the Catholic Common Ground Initiative. It was also published as "Is Christ Divided? Insights from Vatican II for Dealing with Diversity and Disagreement," *Origins* 33 (July 17, 2003).

3. See Christopher Ruddy, "Tomorrow's Catholics: Three Visions of Crisis and Reform: James Carroll, *Toward a New Catholic Church*; George Weigel, *The Courage to Be Catholic*; and Garry Wills, *Why I Am a Catholic*," *The Christian Century* 120 (January 25, 2003): 24–32.

4. John Jay College of Criminal Justice, "The Nature and Scope of the Problem of Sexual Abuse of Minors by Catholic Priests and Deacons in the United States." Available at: http://www.usccb.org/nrb/johnjaystudy.

5. Robert P. Imbelli, "Rediscovering Priesthood in Light of the Eucharist," *Touchstone* (Winter 2003): 9–10, at 9.

6. Greeley, *Priests*, 122.

7. Ibid., 120. See also Stephen J. Rossetti, "Post-Crisis Morale among Priests," *America* 191 (September 13, 2004): 8–10. He reports, on the basis of a survey of over eight hundred priests in eleven dioceses, that 83 percent of priests agree that "my morale is good," but only 40 percent say that "morale in the priesthood is good."

8. Greeley, *Priests*, 120.

9. Peter Steinfels, "Beliefs," *New York Times* (September 24, 2005). Steinfels's statistics on seminarians are drawn from Victor J. Klimoski, Kevin J. O'Neil, and Katarina M. Schuth, *Educating Leaders for Ministry* (Collegeville, MN: Liturgical Press, 2005).

10. Richard John Neuhaus, *Catholic Matters: Confusion, Controversy, and the Splendor of Truth* (New York: Basic Books, 2006), 175–76, 199.

11. Peter Casarella, "Not a Fusion of Liberal and Conservative," *Initiative Report* 7 (June 2003): 3–6, at 6.

12. Philip Murnion, "Priest's Letter to Bishops at Time of His Death," *Origins* 33 (September 4, 2003).

Conference Participants

(Identification as of March 2003)

*Members of the Catholic Common Ground Initiative's
Advisory Committee:*

R. Scott Appleby, director of the University of Notre Dame's
    Joan B. Kroc Institute for International Peace Studies

Sidney Callahan, McKeever Chair of Moral Theology at St.
    John's University, Queens, N.Y.

Peter Casarella, associate professor of systematic theology in
    religious studies at The Catholic University of America,
    Washington, D.C.

Father Cyprian Davis, O.S.B., professor of church history at
    St. Meinrad School of Theology in Indiana

Thomas Donnelly, board member of The Catholic University
    of America, Washington, D.C.

Sister Sharon Euart, R.S.M., consultant on matters of canon
    law

Sister Doris Gottemoeller, R.S.M., senior vice president for
    mission and values integration at Catholic Healthcare
    Partners

Father Robert Imbelli, associate professor of theology at
    Boston College

Ann Chih Lin, assistant professor of public policy and politi-
    cal science in the Gerald R. Ford School of Public Policy
    at the University of Michigan, Ann Arbor

Archbishop Oscar Lipscomb of Mobile, Ala.

Monsignor Philip Murnion, director of New York's National Pastoral Life Center

Archbishop Daniel Pilarczyk of Cincinnati, Ohio

Bishop Ricardo Ramírez, C.S.B., of Las Cruces, N.M.

Sister Katarina Schuth, O.S.F., endowed chair for the social scientific study of religion at the St. Paul Seminary School of Divinity, University of St. Thomas in St. Paul

Staff members Sister Donna Ciangio, O.P., and Sister Catherine Patten, R.S.H.M., coordinator of the Catholic Common Ground Initiative, also attended

Invited Participants:

Chris Alderete, president of the San Antonio Archdiocesan Commission for Women

Father Jeremiah Boland, Chicago archdiocese's delegate for externs and international priests

Father Gerald Brown, S.S., rector-president of Assumption Seminary in San Antonio

Monsignor Neil Connolly, pastor of St. Mary's Church, New York, N.Y.

Ernesto Cortés Jr., southwest regional director of the Industrial Areas Foundation

Father Donald Cozzens, visiting professor of religious studies at John Carroll University in Cleveland

Marilyn Donnelly, advisory council member of the International Poetry Forum

Father Gerald Fogarty, S.J., professor of religious studies and history at the University of Virginia

Father David García, rector of San Fernando Cathedral, San Antonio, Tex.

Paul Griffiths, Arthur Schmitt professor of Catholic studies at the University of Illinois in Chicago

Father Douglas Haefner, pastor of the Catholic Community of St. Matthias in Somerset, N.J.

Father Mark Hession, pastor of Our Lady of Victory in Centerville, Mass.

Monsignor Francis Kelley, pastor of Sacred Heart Parish, Boston

Patricia Kelly, psychologist and founder of Kelly Counseling & Consulting

Father R. J. Cletus Kiley, executive director of the Secretariat for Priestly Life and Ministry, U.S. Conference of Catholic Bishops, Washington, D.C.

Robert Kusenberger Jr., permanent deacon in the San Antonio archdiocese

Carmen Mason, an active member of St. Matthew's Parish, San Antonio

Father Enda McDonagh, Irish moral theologian and lecturer

Sheila McLaughlin, director of the Joseph Bernardin Center for Theology and Ministry at Chicago's Catholic Theological Union

Father William Morell, O.M.I., president of Oblate School of Theology in San Antonio

Father Edward Oakes, S.J., associate professor of theology at Regis University, Denver

Thomas O'Donnell, counsel of Boston law firm Ropes & Gray

Roberto Piña, pastoral team member for the Mexican American Cultural Center in San Antonio

Christopher Ruddy, assistant professor at St. John's University, Collegeville, Minn.

Father Anthony Ruff, O.S.B., instructor of theology, liturgical music, and Gregorian chant at St. John's University, Collegeville, Minn.

Monsignor Dennis Sheehan, pastor of St. Paul Church, Cambridge, Mass.

Father Robert Silva, president of the National Federation of Priests' Councils

Father Thomas Singer, O.M.I., member of the General Council of the Oblates of Mary Immaculate in Rome

Monsignor John Strynkowski, executive director of the U.S. Conference of Catholic Bishops' department of doctrine and pastoral practices

Father Donald Wolf, pastor of Assumption Parish in Duncan, Okla.

Sister Susan Wood, S.C.L., theology professor and associate dean for the School of Theology at St. John's University, Collegeville, Minn.

About the Author

Herder & Herder is honored to welcome Christopher Ruddy again to our house. Dr. Ruddy is an assistant professor of theology at the University of St. Thomas in St. Paul, Minnesota. He taught previously at St. John's University and the College of St. Benedict in Minnesota. A graduate of Yale College and Harvard Divinity School, he received his doctorate in systematic theology from the University of Notre Dame. His writing has appeared in *America, Christian Century, Commonweal, Horizons,* and *Logos*; his article "No Restorationist: Ratzinger's Theological Journey" was a cover story for the June 3, 2005 issue of *Commonweal*. His theological interests include ecclesiology, ecumenism, and the relationship of Christ and culture. His first book, *The Local Church*, appeared in 2006 with Herder & Herder. Dr. Ruddy is presently working on a book on *la nouvelle théologie* and its influence upon Vatican II and contemporary Catholicism. In 2006–2007, he will be a member-in-residence at the Center of Theological Inquiry in Princeton, New Jersey.

A native of New York City, he lives in St. Paul with his wife, Deborah, and their two sons, Peter and Luke.

Of Related Interest

CHRISTOPHER RUDDY
THE LOCAL CHURCH
Tillard and the Future of Catholic Ecclesiology

As Christianity becomes increasingly global in its membership and its practices, how will it deal with increasing tensions between the unity of the faith and the diversity of its expressions? How should the papal ministry of unity be exercised, so that, in the words of Pope John Paul II, "while in no way renouncing what is essential to its mission, [it] is nonetheless open to a new situation"? How can the relationships between local churches and the universal church be improved? Building upon the work of leading theologians over the past two centuries, particularly the Dominican ecumenist and papal consultor Jean-Marie Tillard, Christopher Ruddy, whose writings have appeared in *America, Christian Century, Commonweal,* and *Logos,* offers us *The Local Church,* with signposts to guide the Church as it responds to these and other challenges.

Topics include:
* The relationship of papal primacy and episcopal collegiality
* Inculturation and evangelization
* The quest for Christian unity
* The ecclesiology of Pope Benedict XVI and its future implications
* The centrality of Christology and soteriology to ecclesiology
* Baptism and Eucharist
* Diverse visions of communion ecclesiology

crossroad